GOOD EATING GUIDE

MINI GUIDE TO KILOJOULES AND CALORIES

GW00402045

DR LAUREL MORRIS

LOTHIAN BOOKS

The figures in this guide are based on figures from *Composition of Foods, Australia* AGPS and from information provided by food manufacturers.

A Lothian book
Lothian Publishing Company Pty Ltd
11 Munro Street Port Melbourne Victoria 3207

Copyright © Laurel Morris 1992
First published 1992

National Library of Australia
Cataloguing-in-Publication data

Morris, Laurel.
Good eating guide.

ISBN 0 80591 457 4.
1. Food — Calorific content — Tables.
I. Title.

641.1042

Illustrated by Robert Mancini
Typeset by Bookset
Printed by Australian Print Group
Distributed to newsagents by Gordon and Gotch Limited

CONTENTS

ARE YOU OVERWEIGHT?

Overweight and obesity are associated with a number of health risks in addition to the aesthetic drawbacks. Use a combination of the following tests to see whether you should be losing weight.

TABLES

The most common method of assessing your degree of overweight is by comparing your weight to recommended healthy weights for men and women, depending on your height and build. You are considered 'overweight' if you are more than 10 per cent over the ideal weight for your height and frame, and 'obese' if you exceed 20 per cent. The tables can't account for your own individual combination of bone and muscle sizes and shapes, but can be a good guide.

HOW TO DECIDE YOUR FRAME

	Small	Medium	Large
WOMEN	**Small**	**Medium**	**Large**
Wrist	under 13.5 cm	13.5 to 16 cm	Over 16 cm
MEN	**Small**	**Medium**	**Large**
Hand-span	under 17 cm	17 to 23.5 cm	over 23.5 cm
Chest	under 91 cm	91 to 109 cm	over 109 cm
Shoulders	under 42 cm	42 to 52 cm	over 52 cm
Foot	under 20 cm	20 to 25 cm	over 25 cm

IDEAL WEIGHTS

WOMEN — AGE 25 AND OVER — INDOOR CLOTHING
(16–25 years: subtract 0.5 kg for each year under 25.)

Height (no shoes)		Small	Medium	Large
145	(4' 9")	43–6 kg	45–50 kg	48–55 kg
148	(4' 10")	44–8	46–51	49–57
150	(4' 11")	45–9	47–53	51–8
153	(5' 0")	46–50	49–54	52–9
155	(5' 1")	48–51	50–5	53–61
158	(5' 2")	49–53	51–7	55–63
160	(5' 3")	50–4	53–9	57–64
163	(5' 4")	52–6	54–61	59–66
165	(5' 5")	54–8	56–63	60–8
168	(5' 6")	55–9	58–65	62–70
170	(5' 7")	57–61	60–7	64–72
173	(5' 8")	59–63	62–9	66–74
175	(5' 9")	61–5	63–70	68–76
178	(5' 10")	63–7	65–72	69–79

MEN — INDOOR CLOTHING

158	(5' 2")	52–6	55–60	59–65
160	(5' 3")	53–7	56–62	60–7
163	(5' 4")	55–8	58–63	61–9
165	(5' 5")	56–60	59–65	63–71
168	(5' 6")	58–62	61–7	64–73
170	(5' 7")	60–4	63–9	67–75
173	(5' 8")	62–6	64–71	68–77
175	(5' 9")	64–8	66–73	70–9
178	(5' 10")	65–70	68–75	72–81
180	(5' 11")	67–72	70–7	74–84
183	(6' 0")	69–74	72–9	76–86
185	(6' 1")	71–6	74–82	78–88
188	(6' 2")	73–8	76–84	81–90
190	(6' 3")	74–9	78–86	83–93

BODY MASS INDEX (BMI)

Your BMI correlates very closely with your lean body mass, which is the percentage of your total weight made up of muscle and bone. Therefore, it will give you a very good indication of your proportion of body fat. To calculate your BMI, use this formula:

$$BMI = \frac{weight\ in\ kilograms}{height\ (in\ metres) \times height\ (in\ metres)}$$

For example, if you are 167 centimetres (1.67 metres) tall and weigh 85 kilograms, your BMI = 85 divided by (1.67 × 1.67) = 30.48.

A healthy BMI is considered to be between 20 and 25. Over 25 is considered overweight and over 30 is considered obese. A BMI below 20 reflects underweight which is also associated with increased health risks.

PINCH TEST

A simple pinch test involves pinching a fold of skin with its subcutaneous fat away from the body. Try this on your stomach below your ribs. A skin fold thicker than 2.5 cm for a man or 3 cm for a woman suggests overweight.

MIRROR TEST

Perhaps this is the simplest and most telling way of seeing whether you need to lose weight and/or tone up.

Simply strip off and stand in front of a full length mirror. Do you look fat? Do you bulge in the wrong places? If so, it's time to do something about it.

METRIC CONVERSIONS

kg	st. lb	kg	st. lb
0.5	0.1	66.5	10.7
1.0	0.2¼	68.0	10.10
6.4	1.0	69.7	11.0
12.7	2.0	71.0	11.3
19.0	3.0	72.8	11.7
25.4	4.0	74.2	11.10
31.8	5.0	76.0	12.0
38.2	6.0	77.3	12.3
41.5	6.7	79.0	12.7
44.5	7.0	80.5	12.10
47.5	7.7	82.3	13.0
51.7	8.0	85.5	13.7
52.0	8.3	88.5	14.0
54.0	8.7	91.7	14.7
55.3	8.10	95.0	15.0
57.0	9.0	98.0	15.7
58.5	9.3	101.2	16.0
60.3	9.7	108.5	17.0
61.5	9.10	114.5	18.0
63.5	10.0	121.0	19.0
64.8	10.3	127.3	20.0

TEN STEPS FOR HEALTHY EATING

1 **Eat a balanced diet across all food groups**   Eat a wide variety of foods. This helps ensure that you receive adequate nutrition.

2 **Reduce the amount of simple sugars you eat**   These are high energy foods with low nutritional value. Try adding less when preparing foods and beware of the added sugar in processed foods. All sugars, except sorbitol, give a burst of energy followed by a slump leaving you feeling crabby and wanting another 'fix'.

3 **Increase complex carbohydrates in your diet**   This includes fruit, vegetables and cereals, which are digested more slowly than simple carbohydrates (sugars) and provide a steady release of energy.

4 **Reduce consumption of fats**   Fats are high energy sources and are hidden in many processed foods. Try trimming the visible fat off meat, removing the skin from poultry, finding a low-fat substitute spread for butter and margarine, cutting down on hard and processed cheeses and developing a taste for skim milk.

5 **Replace saturated fats with unsaturated fats**   Saturated fats, found in animal products such as meat, cheese and butter, tend to increase the levels of cholesterol and triglycerides in the blood. This in turn contributes to coronary heart disease and the risk of stroke.

6 **Decrease salt intake**   Stop adding salt to your foods and avoid processed foods with added salt. Salt is associated with high blood pressure and may increase water retention in your body.

7 **Drink more water**   Water is the most essential nutrient of all and a healthy thirst quencher. Avoid drinks that provide unneeded energy, like soft drinks, and limit caffeine-containing drinks.

8 **Drink alcohol in moderation**   Alcohol is a high energy/low nutritional value food. For both weight control and health reasons, consider alcohol a luxury to be enjoyed in moderation.

9 **Eat protein in moderation**   Proteins supply essential nutrients and are good for long-term hunger control, but are not needed in large amounts and are often associated with unwanted saturated fats.

10 **Decrease your consumption of take-away and processed foods**   These foods often have high levels of hidden salt, sugar and fat and the processing of foods removes much of the vitamin, mineral and fibre content. Opt for home-prepared meals made from fresh ingredients.

FAD DIETS

The traditionally accepted method of losing weight has been 'the diet' and we must have lost count of the number of varieties of fad diets around. The problems with any 'diet' are:

1 They are **restrictive** — often suggesting a narrow variety of food choices which can promote an unbalanced and unhealthy dietary intake.

2 They are **short-term** and seen as a quick fix for weight problems that have often been longstanding. If you have a problem with your weight it will require ongoing, lifelong strategies to control it.

3 Diets involving restricted food intake actually **create** a weight problem. Approximately two-thirds of the energy used by your body goes towards maintaining bodily functions — this is determined by your metabolic rate. The restricted energy intake of a diet influences your body to actually lower its metabolic rate and become more energy efficient, thus cancelling out much of the effects of the diet. This drop in metabolic rate with restricted eating is from 15–30 per cent; dropping more in those who already have a low metabolic rate, which includes a lot of overweight people. This drop in metabolic rate can cancel out any weight loss effect you initially achieved on the diet and explains why some diets seem to just stop working.

An additional problem with diets and metabolic rate is that your metabolic rate, lowered by the diet, **remains low** even when you go off the diet and this contributes to an increased rate of weight gain. And so the cycle of weight gain and loss goes on and your body tends to adapt by dropping its metabolic rate faster with each successive diet. (See our section on Exercise and Metabolic Rate on page 18.)

EATING PLANS

It is important to ensure that your diet is balanced across all food groups in appropriate proportions. This becomes even more vital when your total daily energy intake is low.

You should first decide on an appropriate daily kilojoule/Calorie intake for your height and desired weight, then note the suggested amounts to be included from each of the major food groups. It doesn't really matter what foods you choose (they should fit your preferences and tastes) as long as the total kilojoules/Calories for the food group is close to that suggested. For each of the food groups draw up a list of possible food combinations that total to the suggested amount, then draw upon these lists to design your own daily menus.

The example menus are suggestions only and indicate possible ways of covering all of the food groups. It is most important that you learn to design your own balanced menus that fit your tastes and preferences so you can maintain healthy eating in the long term.

4200 kJ (1000 Cals) a day plan

kJ	Cals	
475	110	Fruit
540	130	Vegetables
890	210	Cereals/Bread
940	225	Meat/Fish/Protein
670	160	Milk
375	90	Fats
310	75	Luxuries

For example:

Breakfast: ½ glass (100 ml) orange juice
30 g cereal
½ cup (125 ml) skim milk
1 slice wholemeal toast
1 tsp butter/margarine

Lunch: 1 small apple
2 crispbreads
¼ cup tuna
1 medium tomato
1 tsp butter/margarine or 20 g cottage cheese

Dinner: 100 g lean steak, grilled
1 small potato (steamed)
1 small zucchini (steamed)
1 small carrot (steamed)
2 cm slice fresh pineapple
1 small glass wine

100 ml milk for tea and coffee throughout the day

5000 kJ (1200 Cals) a day plan

kJ	Cals	
545	130	Fruit
585	140	Vegetables
1250	300	Cereals/Bread
1250	300	Meat/Fish/Protein
670	160	Milk
380	90	Fats
320	75	Luxuries

For example:

Breakfast: ½ grapefruit
   30 g cereal
   ½ cup (125 ml) skim milk
   1 slice wholemeal toast
   1 tsp butter/margerine
Lunch: Small bunch grapes (60 g)
   1 sandwich with slice cheese and tomato
   Butter/Margarine on sandwich
Dinner: 3 slices roast beef (150 g)
   ¼ cob sweetcorn
   90 g butternut pumpkin
   60 g green beans
   1 small pear (90 g)
   30 ml brandy with low-joule mixer
100 ml milk for tea and coffee during the day

6350 kJ (1500 Cals) a day plan

kJ	Cals	
630	150	Fruit
835	200	Vegetables
1460	350	Cereals/Bread
1880	450	Meat/Fish/Protein
670	160	Milk
565	135	Fat
310	75	Luxuries

For example:

Breakfast: 1 small banana
   30 g muesli
   125 ml skim milk
   1 slice wholemeal toast
   1 tsp butter/margarine
Lunch: 4 crispbreads with cottage cheese and salad (grated carrot, lettuce, alfalfa)
   1 slice Virginia ham
   2 small nectarines
Dinner: 1 chicken fillet, grilled
   1 boiled potato
   1 floret cauliflower
   ½ cup carrot
   1 floret broccoli
   1 baked apple
   1 fun-sized Bounty bar
100 ml milk in tea and coffee during the day

A balanced diet for both good health and weight control is what you should plan for the rest of your life — not just as a short-term measure. Therefore, your diet must be palatable, practical, flexible and nutritionally balanced, varying only in its total energy content to achieve weight loss, or maintenance, depending on your current goals.

7600 kJ (1800 Cals) a day plan

kJ	Cals	
1000	240	Fruit
1250	300	Vegetables
1750	420	Cereals/Bread
1870	450	Meat/Fish/Protein
670	160	Milk
750	180	Fats
310	75	Luxuries

For example:

Breakfast: ½ glass (125 ml) orange juice
½ cup stewed fruit
30 g cereal
100 ml milk
1 slice wholegrain toast
1 tsp butter/margarine
1 soft boiled egg

Lunch: 1 sandwich with ham, cheese, tomato, lettuce, sprouts, grated carrot
1 medium apple

Dinner: 250 g fish fillet, grilled
½ cup celery, tomato, onion
½ cup green peas
1 scoop frozen yoghurt
100 g strawberries
15 g chocolate

100 ml milk in tea and coffee during the day

8400 kJ (2000 Cals) a day plan

kJ	Cals	
1000	240	Fruit
1200	285	Vegetables
2000	475	Cereals/Bread
2200	525	Meat/Fish/Protein
650	155	Milk
750	180	Fats
600	145	Luxuries

For example:

Breakfast: ½ grapefruit
30 g muesli
½ cup (125 ml) skim milk
6 canned apricot halves, drained
2 slices wholemeal toast
2 tsp butter/margarine

Lunch: 1 croissant with 100 g tuna
1 tossed salad — lettuce, tomato, carrot, cucumber, sprouts and 1 egg
1 tbsp dressing
1 banana

Dinner: 200 ml pumpkin soup
250 g lamb cubes skewered with peppers, mushroom and tomato
¾ cup steamed rice with spinach
½ cup carrot (steamed)
3 baby squash (steamed)
¼ large rockmelon
1 scoop frozen yoghurt
120 ml glass wine
1 fun-sized Mars bar

100 ml milk in tea and coffee during the day

DAILY ENERGY REQUIREMENTS

	Weight		Kilojoules required	
	kg	st:lb	18–35 years	over 35 years
Women	45	7:0	7,100	6,500
	51	8:0	7,550	6,900
	54	8:7	8,150	7,550
	57	9:0	8,350	7,750
	60	9:6	8,900	7,950
	65	10:3	9,200	8,350
	70	11:0	9,650	8,800
	75	11:11	10,050	9,200
Men	60	9:6	10,700	9,850
	65	10:3	11,100	10,250
	70	11:0	11,700	10,700
	75	11:11	12,150	11,100
	80	12:8	12,750	11,700
	85	13:5	13,400	12,350
	90	14:2	14,050	12,750

Variations for different activity levels

inactive (e.g. bed-ridden)	subtract 2,900 kJ
average (e.g. clerical job, housework)	no change
active (e.g. trades work, heavy housework)	add 1,650 kJ
very active (e.g. labouring)	add 3,750 kJ

Variations for pregnancy

during second half of pregnancy	add 650 kJ
while breast feeding	add 3,750 kJ

Average daily energy requirements for children

6 months– 1 yr	200 kJ per 0.5 kg (1 lb) of body weight	11–15 yrs	7,100 to 10,450 kJ for girls; 8,350 to 12,550 kJ for boys
1–3 yrs	4,600 to 5,850 kJ	15–18 yrs	6,300 to 9,200 kJ for girls;
3–7 yrs	5,850 to 7,100 kJ		8,350 to 12,550 kJ for boys
7–11 yrs	7,100 to 9,200 kJ		

HEALTHY ALTERNATIVES TO UNHEALTHY EATING

All behaviour generally has identifiable reasons, and learning to pinpoint and address those reasons will help you with unwise eating behaviour. Those reasons may be triggers, or things which prompt you to eat; or consequences — the effects you are trying to achieve from eating. So, unwise eating — making poor food choices or eating too much — often occurs for reasons other than hunger. Partly it may simply reflect the enjoyment food can provide, but frequently eating can become a way of coping with bad feelings. Smoking and drinking are other health-reducing behaviours which are often triggered by bad feelings and give a short-term boost to your emotions.

Identify triggers and consequences

The process of self-monitoring, outlined in *Putting Yourself in Control* on page 15, is designed to help you identify the triggers and consequences of your unwise eating, smoking and drinking. Once you have identified these you can look for alternative ways of responding to those triggers or achieving those consequences. These will become your **healthy alternatives** and it is important to strengthen them to give you long-term control over health-reducing behaviour.

HEALTHY ALTERNATIVE BEHAVIOURS

This table lists the common triggers and consequences of health-reducing behaviours, along with their healthy alternatives. Work out which triggers and consequences are influencing your unwise eating, drinking or smoking. Then you will know which alternative behaviours you will need to acquire or strengthen to resist the triggers or achieve the desired consequences. Your best chance of establishing and maintaining healthy behaviours will come from taking a broad approach such as this.

Trigger	Desired consequences	Healthy alternative
Tension, anxiety	Relaxation	Mental relaxation, anxiety management
Fears, memories, intrusive thoughts	Comfort	Mental relaxation
Depression	Escape from feeling bad	Depression management
Loneliness	To feel good, to stop feeling bad	Loneliness management, social skills
Relationship problems	To forget problems To stop feeling bad	Relationship enhancement
Anger, frustration	To build courage, reduce frustration	Anger management, assertion skills
Shyness, social anxiety	Social ease	Mental relaxation, social skills
Pressure from others	Acceptance, avoiding conflict	Assertion
Insomnia	Sleep	Insomnia management
Boredom	Stimulation	Activity building

For more information about healthy alternative behaviours see *The Truth about Success and Motivation* and *Your Good Health* also written by Dr Laurel Morris and Dr Bob Montgomery.

PUTTING YOURSELF IN CONTROL

There are three basic techniques to help you in establishing your sensible eating and weight management programme: self-monitoring, building motivation and surviving relapses.

STEPS FOR SELF-MONITORING

1 Keep a small notebook which can fit easily into your pocket or bag.
2 Keep the records for a typical week as this should be sufficient to pick up the major influences on your eating.
3 Start a new page for each day and rule it up with these headings: **WHEN, WHAT, WHERE, THOUGHTS AND FEELINGS**
4 Under WHEN, record the time you were eating or drinking.
5 Under WHAT, record what you ate or drank, how it was prepared and include the kilojoule total.
6 Under WHERE, record details of the situation, your location, what else you were doing, who you were with.
7 Finally, under THOUGHTS AND FEELINGS, record thoughts and feelings that seem to be associated with your eating. These may change while you are eating, so record them all.

STEPS FOR BUILDING MOTIVATION

1 Identify the changes you wish to make in your health-related behaviour. These changes should be precise and clear, so there is no room for doubt about whether you have achieved them.
2 Identify possible rewards and penalties that will act as incentives for you.
3 Write out your contract, putting in your goals, rewards and penalties. It's a good idea to use two contracts within the one form: a short-term weekly contract to stick to your goals, and a long-term contract to help you maintain the behaviour changes.
4 Sign and date the contract and maybe get your spouse or a friend to witness it. If you have your spouse or a friend helping, it is important that they see their role as encouraging you with praise when you keep your contract rather than nagging you when you do not.
5 Draw up a tally sheet and start recording your progress, administering rewards and penalties as you go.

EXAMPLE OF A CONTRACT

I promise myself that each week I will stick to my healthy eating plan.
(Attach your plan.)
Each week that I keep this contract I will reward myself with a new
cassette or $10 in my special purpose account.
Each week that I don't keep this contract I will penalise myself by missing
my favourite television programme.
When I have kept this contract for three months my grand reward will be a
new jacket.
I recognise that this contract is a promise I make myself to achieve
something I want but expect to find difficult. If I cheat on this I only cheat
myself.

Signed .... **Date** ....

MANAGING RELAPSES

It is important to regard relapses as an occasional but unavoidable occurrence, because telling yourself that you must *never* relapse sets you up for really bad relapses. If a relapse leads you to overreact negatively ('Oh no! I've blown it! I knew I could never do it!') you are setting yourself up for a really big relapse ('What's the point? I give up. I may as well eat all of it now!'). Since many of the factors that encourage unhealthy behaviour are environmental influences such as advertising and the availability of unhealthy products, you cannot isolate yourself from them totally. Further, you won't change your entrenched habits instantly and permanently. So it makes sense to expect to relapse occasionally. The key is not to overreact, but to try some relapse management.

PLANNED RELAPSES

There are bound to be times when you wish to eat and drink freely outside the bounds of sensible eating and drinking guidelines. For these (occasional) times you can *plan* to relapse, interpret it realistically, and return to your everyday sensible programme straight afterwards.

EXERCISE AND METABOLIC RATE

The role of exercise in weight loss and maintenance has been misunderstood. Traditionally, suggestions have been made about how much energy you could burn up by doing various activities and exercise. But the truth is that you won't burn up much extra energy directly while you are exercising unless you are able and willing to exercise very hard for quite long periods.

The vital contribution of exercise to weight loss is through its effects on your resting metabolic rate (RMR). Moderate exercise increases your RMR by about 10 per cent, and this increase continues up to twelve hours afterwards. This increase does lessen if you exercise consistently and increase your level of fitness, but that means that exercise is helping to maintain a new, higher RMR, not that it is losing its effectiveness.

TRAINING PULSE RATES (per minute)

AGE	TPR1 (1st 8 weeks)	TPR2 (2nd 8 weeks)	TPR3 (3rd 8 weeks)	TPR4 (maint'ce)
Under 30	120	140	150	150–160
30–44	110	130	140	140–150
45–60	100	120	130	130–140
Over 60	100	110	120	120–130

AEROBIC EXERCISE

Aerobic exercise is any activity that increases your heart and breathing rates by increasing the body's demand for oxygen. The major guidelines for effective aerobic exercise in order to achieve a training effect are:

1 It should **involve large muscle groups** such as the legs and arms and involve rhythmic contractions.

2 It must be done **frequently enough** so that the benefits of an increased training effect are not lost between workouts.

3 Each workout should be **long enough** to achieve a training effect. This involves continuous exercise for at least 20 minutes. There is not a large benefit in extending the workout beyond 30 minutes.

4 The exercise should be **vigorous enough** to involve the whole body and achieve a training effect. This level can be gauged by your body's individual reaction to the chosen exercise. Ideally the aerobic exercise should be increasing your heart rate and pulse to around 60–70 per cent of its maximum. This rate is known as your **training pulse rate (TPR)** and will vary depending on your age and fitness level. Refer to the table to determine the pulse rate you should be aiming for.

BENEFITS OF EXERCISE

- An improvement in the efficiency of your heart, lungs, and blood system so you can cope with higher levels of physical activity.
- An increase in muscle strength and joint strength and flexibility.
- Greater endurance capacity, less fatigue.
- Reduced blood fat and cholesterol levels.
- Contributes to an overall stress management programme.
- Improved posture.
- May help reduce mild hypertension.
- Contributes to weight loss and maintenance.

ALCOHOL AND CAFFEINE

It is important to consider what you drink for weight control and nutritional purposes, especially to watch the kilojoules and other additives in many drinks such as fruit juice, milk and soft drinks. However some people drink to obtain the effect of a drug and too much can cause harm. The two most widely used and socially acceptable drugs are caffeine and alcohol.

CAFFEINE

Caffeine has a stimulant effect and provides a 'lift'. Moderate caffeine consumption over long periods of time has not been shown to have any harmful effects, although it is addictive. Too much caffeine can cause insomnia, stomach upsets, frequent urination, tremors, nervousness and irritability.

Individuals vary in their sensitivity to caffeine, so you should adjust the amounts in the following guidelines if you find that you have any side effects at these levels. Moderate caffeine drinking is a level at which the negative side effects are unlikely. For most people, up to 300 mg of caffeine per day should present no problems. The amount of caffeine in tea and coffee will vary depending on the variety used, length of brewing time and size of the cup, but below is a rough guide to moderate caffeine drinking.

ALCOHOL

Excessive alcohol drinking is not only a health risk, but can also contribute a lot of unwanted kilojoules minus any nutritional benefit. However, most people who drink do not drink to great excess and do not experience alcohol-related problems.

RECOMMENDED CAFFEINE INTAKE

Type of drink	Caffeine per cup (mg)	No. of cups (per day)
Brewed coffee	100	3
Instant coffee	60	5
Tea	50	6
Cola	40	7

The harm from excessive drinking can take various forms and if it is affecting your health, work, finances, family or causing you emotional problems you should take some constructive steps to reduce your alcohol intake.

Excessive drinking can affect your liver, brain, kidneys, resistance to infection and cause loss of sensations, tremors and tingling. It is estimated that one in five hospital beds are occupied by people with problems related to alcohol.

Women are more susceptible to the health damaging effects of excessive drinking. This is partly because women absorb alcohol faster than men, probably because of metabolic differences, and thus reach a high blood alcohol concentration (BAC) faster. But mostly it is because of differences in their body size and composition. Firstly, women tend to weigh less than men, therefore will reach a higher BAC for the same number of drinks. Secondly, because women have a higher proportion of their body as fat and less water there is less water in their bodies to dilute the alcohol and they wind up with a higher BAC.

It is not known exactly why women are more susceptible to alcohol damage — it may be due to hormonal differences or patterns of drinking — but studies indicate that women are at greater risk of liver damage, brain damage, ulcers and drinking-related cancers than men.

If you wish to learn more about establishing a sensible drinking programme, I suggest *Your Good Health* by Dr Bob Mongomery and Dr Laurel Morris, published by Lothian Books.

DRINKING GUIDELINES
Standard drinks
(drinks that contain 8–10 grams of pure alcohol)
Beer (4.8–5% alcohol), 1 glass 285 ml
Light beer (3.3% alcohol), 1 can, 375 ml
Wine, 1 glass, 120 ml
Port or sherry, 1 small glass, 60 ml
Spirits, 1 nip, 30 ml
Cider, 1 glass, 285 ml
Wine cooler, 1 glass, 285 ml

Recommended limits
(standard drinks)

MEN
No more than 4 per day
No more than 28 per week
No more than 8 as a special occasion limit

WOMEN
No more than 2 per day
No more than 14 per week
No more than 4 as a special occasion limit

FIBRE

Dietary fibre includes food components that pass through most of the digestive tract undigested. Some components of dietary fibre are absorbed in the large intestine. There is evidence to suggest that a diet high in fibre may help treat or prevent disorders including constipation, diverticulitis, irritable bowel syndrome and haemorrhoids. A diet high in fat and cholesterol and low in dietary fibre and complex carbohydrates has been implicated in the development of bowel cancer. Cancers of the lung, breast, uterus, prostate and pancreas may also be influenced by such a diet. Fibre also appears to slow the rate of absorption of sugars from food, so it is beneficial in treating diabetes. Certain types of fibre, pectins from fruit and vegetable gums, are thought to contribute to lowering blood cholesterol levels, therefore reducing coronary risk.

Dietary fibre exists only in foods of plant origin, so to increase fibre you should increase your intake of fruits, vegetables and cereals. It is generally accepted that most Australians need to increase their fibre consumption to between 30 and 50 g per day.

TEN STEPS FOR INCREASING FIBRE

1 Increase the amount of fruit in your diet.
2 Increase the amount of vegetables in your diet.
3 Increase cereal products, which are good sources of complex carbohydrate.
4 Minimise peeling of fruit and vegetables.
5 Choose wholegrain breads instead of white breads.
6 Choose wholegrain flours instead of refined flours — they have three times as much fibre.
7 Decrease your consumption of processed foods. Processing removes fibre (along with many other nutrients).
8 Eat whole fruit instead of drinking fruit juices; this has the same calories, but the benefit of added fibre.
9 Add an extra serve of vegetables to your plate; have a smaller serve of meat.
10 Investigate new recipes involving wholegrain foods, pulses, beans and vegetables.

CALCIUM AND OSTEOPOROSIS

Calcium is the most abundant mineral in the body with most of it in the bones and teeth. The calcium in the soft tissues is necessary for blood clotting, the functioning of muscles and nerve tissues, and for the manufacture of enzymes in the body. During periods of growth the demand for calcium increases, so children, adolescents and pregnant and lactating women need additional calcium intake.

OSTEOPOROSIS

Osteoporosis is a decrease in bone density resulting in thinner bones which are more susceptible to breaking. Osteoporosis is common in postmenopausal women and particularly affects the wrists, hips and spine. A curvature of the spine caused by collapsing vertebrae, or dowager's hump, can result.

Periodontal disease is also associated with osteoporosis. Pockets created around the teeth, because of loss of bone in the jaw, are susceptible to infection. This condition can eventually result in the loss of teeth.

Symptoms include recurring night-time leg cramps, heavy plaque or calculus on your teeth, and osteoarthritic changes in the joints.

TEN STEPS FOR FIGHTING OSTEOPOROSIS

1 Increase calcium-rich foods Milk, yoghurt and cheese are the best sources. Other good sources include: canned sardines, pilchards and salmon (if the bones are eaten); prawns; and green leafy vegetables — broccoli, silverbeet, spinach.

2 Increase exercise Load bearing exercise such as aerobics, walking, jogging or cycling are helpful.

3 Ensure vitamin D is adequate A supplement is usually unnecessary. You should obtain sufficient vitamin D if you have a balanced diet and some exposure to sunlight.

4 Moderate phosphate-rich foods Eat red meats in moderation and cut down on all soft drinks.

5 Moderate alcohol consumption Keep within the healthy limits suggested in the section on Alcohol and Caffeine on page 20.

6 Decrease simple sugars Cut down on confectionery, sweet biscuits, cake and soft drinks.

continued

23

7 Avoid smoking The contribution of smoking towards osteoporosis is only one of its health-damaging effects. No level of smoking is safe.

8 Manage your stress effectively High stress levels produce hormonal shifts in your body — many of which are not yet fully understood. Managing your stress levels will also help you fight osteoporosis.

9 Develop new interests involving physical activity Challenging or interesting physical activities can be rewarding in themselves and will help maintain bone density.

10 Consider hormone replacement therapy See your doctor and talk about hormone replacement therapy if you believe you may be susceptible to the risk of osteoporosis.

DAILY CALCIUM INTAKE

	milligrams
0–6 months	360
6 months–1 year	540
1–10 years	800
11–18 years	1200
19 years and over	800
Postmenopausal women	1200
Pregnant and lactating women	1200

CALCIUM GUIDE

	Calcium mg
BEVERAGES	
Beer, 250 ml	3
Cocoa powder, 2 tsp, 10 g	15
Coffee, brewed, 250 ml	5
Malted milk powder, 2 tsp, 10 g	33
Milo, 2 tsp, 10 g	47
Ovaltine, 2 tsp, 10 g	23
Soft drinks, average, 250 ml	12
Wine, average, 120 ml	12
CEREALS	
Biscuits, 1 average	22
Bread, 1 slice, wholemeal or brown, 25 g	8
1 slice, white, 25 g	5
Pita, 25 g	5
Roll, wholemeal or brown, 35 g	11
Roll, white, 35 g	7
Breakfast cereals, 30 g	
Corn flakes	1
Muesli, Swiss style	31
Muesli, toasted	14
Rice bubbles	2
Special K	17
Flour, 1 cup, 100 g	
Wholemeal	40
Corn	20
Plain	20
Self-raising	90
Soya	220
EGGS	
Egg, raw, boiled, poached, 55 g	50
Scrambled with milk, 100 g	60

	mg
Omelette, 2 eggs with 30 g cheese	330

FATS, OILS, BUTTER, MARGARINE
All have negligible amounts

FISH AND SEAFOODS
	mg
Anchovies, 45 g	75
Crabmeat, 100 g	170
Fish paste, 30 g	130
Mussels, oysters, 1 doz, 120 g	200
Prawns, 6 boiled, 120 g	150
Salmon, average, canned, 100 g	310
Sardines, 1 can, 60 g	460
Scallops, 10 steamed, 100 g	120
Tuna, 100 g	7
Whiting, steamed, 100 g	20

FRUIT
	mg
Apple, 1 medium	3
Apricots, 3 medium, fresh	20
Dried, 100 g	67
Avocado, ½, 100 g	20
Banana, 100 g	7
Blackberries, 100 g	60
Cherries, 20 medium	10
Figs, 2 fresh, 75 g	23
2 dried, 40 g	30
Grapefruit, ½ average, 100 g	8
Kiwifruit, 1 medium, 60 g	15
Mandarin, 1 average, 50 g	18
Mango, 1 average, 100 g	10
Nectarine, 1 average, 40 g	2
Orange, 1 average, 130 g	40
Peach, 1 average, 120 g	7
Pear, 1 average, 120 g	7
Pineapple, ½ × 3 cm slice	20
Plums, 3 average, 100 g	20
Rhubarb, raw, 100 g	26
Strawberries, 10 large, 100 g	20

GRAINS, PULSES, BEANS
	mg
Cannellini beans, canned, 100 g	46
Chickpeas, canned, 100 g	45
Kidney beans, dried, 100 g	95
Lentils, dried, 100 g	73
Lima beans, dried, 100 g	55
Soya beans, dried, 100 g	180
Split peas, dried, 100 g	42

MEAT AND MEAT PRODUCTS
	mg
Average all types, 100 g	10

MILK AND MILK PRODUCTS
Milk — fresh and UHT
	mg
Whole, 200 ml	240
Fat reduced, 200 ml	290
Skim, 200 ml	260
High protein skim, 200 ml	325
Goat's, 200 ml	260
Human, 200 ml	60
Flavoured milk, 200 ml	220
Soy, 220 ml	10

Evaporated and condensed
Whole, 30 ml	280
Skim, 30 ml	380

Dried and powdered
Whole, 1 tbsp, 12 g	150
Skim, 1 tbsp, 10 g	105

Yoghurt
Plain, natural, 200 g	290
Non-fat, natural, 200 g	260
Flavoured, 200 g	260
Non-fat, flavoured, 200 g	260

Cheeses
Camembert, 30 g	120
Cheddar, 30 g	240
Cheese spread, 30 g	150

	mg		mg
Cottage, 30 g	20	Garlic bread, 50 g	35
Cream cheese, 30 g	30	Hamburger, plain, 100 g	21
Danish blue, 30 g	175	With bacon, 100 g	20
Edam, 30 g	220	With cheese, 100 g	83
Parmesan, 30 g	370	McDonalds, big Mac, 200 g	150
Processed, 30 g	210	Cheeseburger	110
Ricotta, 30 g	100	Fillet 'o fish	80
Swiss, 30 g	280	McFeast	130
		McMuffin with egg	200
Cream		McMuffin with sausage and	
Pure, 35%, 30 ml	20	egg	150
Reduced fat, 25%, 30 ml	30	Sundae	220
Sour cream, 35%, 30 ml	20	Milk shake, 350 ml	420
Sour, reduced fat, 25%, 30 ml	40	Quarter pounder with cheese	180
Sour cream dip, 30 ml	40	Pizza, Pizza Hut, 100 g	150
Thickened, 35%, 30 ml	17	With extra cheese, 100 g	240
SAUCES, SPREADS, CONDIMENTS		**VEGETABLES**	
Fish paste, 10 g	28	Artichoke, 100 g	20
Treacle, 30 g	150	Asparagus, 100 g	10
Vegemite, 3 g	3	Beans, green, boiled, 100 g	40
Negligible amounts in other spreads		Kidney, 100 g	70
		Broccoli, 100 g	80
SEEDS AND NUTS		Cabbage, 100 g	50
Almonds, 12, 20 g	50	Carrots, 100 g	40
Brazil nuts, 5, 20 g	36	Cauliflower, 100 g	20
Cashews, 10, 20 g	9	Celery, 100 g	50
Hazel nuts, 13, 20 g	3	Parsley, 10 g	33
Macadamia, 9, 20 g	10	Peas, 100 g	30
Peanuts, 25, 20 g	12	Potato, boiled, baked, 100 g	8
Pistachio, 30, 20 g	26	Mashed with milk	40
Sesame seeds, 20 g	232	Pumpkin, 100 g	40
Walnuts, 5, 20 g	12	Silverbeet, 100 g	70
Tahini spread, 50 g	165	Spinach, 100 g	190
		Tomato, 100 g	10
TAKE-AWAY FOODS		Turnip, 100 g	60
Chiko roll, 100 g	27		
Dim sims, 3, 100 g	67		

FATS AND OILS

The major types of fats are *triglycerides, cholesterols and phospholipids*. These fats contain fatty acids which can be *saturated, polyunsaturated or monounsaturated*.

Saturated fatty acids come mainly from animal sources — particularly ruminant animals such as cattle and sheep. Saturated fats tend to increase the amount of cholesterol and triglycerides in the blood which in turn increase the risk of hardening of the arteries.

Polyunsaturated fats come mainly from plant sources and include vegetable oils and margarine. These fats tend to reduce cholesterol levels in the blood. Another polyunsaturated fatty acid, omega-3-eicosapentaenoic acid (EPA for short!) is contained mainly in cold-water fish, such as sardines, herring and cod, and is used by our bodies to manufacture a substance which prevents blood cells called platelets from sticking together and forming clots. This reduces the risk of heart attacks and strokes.

Monounsaturated fats, such as in olive oil and peanut products, tend to leave cholesterol levels in the blood unchanged. However, cultures which traditionally use monounsaturated fats in their diet have a low incidence of coronary heart disease.

CHOLESTEROL

Cholesterol is a substance resembling fat found only in animal tissues where it forms a part of all animal cell walls and is also used by animals in the production of certain hormones. A problem arises when cholesterol levels are high in the blood and it tends to accumulate on the inner walls of the arteries — gradually thickening (hardening) the blood vessels and inhibiting the blood flow (atherosclerosis). Arteries supplying the heart, brain, eyes, sex organs, legs and gut are commonly affected. This may cause angina pain and heart attacks, strokes, loss of eyesight, erectile impotence, leg pain and gangrene, and intestinal cramps. The health risks of a high cholesterol level are greater when it is associated with high blood pressure and/or smoking.

Dietary cholesterol accounts for only 10–20 per cent of your total blood cholesterol. The rest is manufactured in the body by the liver and intestines so dietary restriction may play only a small part in reducing blood cholesterol levels. Also, it appears that some individuals have a greater tendency for high blood cholesterol levels than others.

HDL and LDL

Cholesterol actually comes in two forms:

1 High density lipoproteins (HDL)
2 Low density lipoproteins (LDL).

HDL is actually beneficial in the body as it acts as a garbage collector picking up atherosclerotic deposits, whereas LDL tends to deposit on the artery walls. Some cholesterol tests, such as in shopping centres, do not make a distinction between the two types of cholesterol. So if you have your level checked do question whether it will show the ratio of LDL to HDL. A ratio of 5:1 is considered to indicate an average risk of coronary heart disease, while a ratio of 3:1 would indicate half the average risk. Unfortunately, most people with raised cholesterol levels generally have more LDL. So, for health reasons, it is desirable to lower overall cholesterol levels, but increase the proportion of HDL. A low-fat, high fibre, nutritious and balanced diet is the best approach here.

One good thing to know about cholesterol is that shellfish, once thought to be a high source of cholesterol, have been found to contain a different kind of fat which does not have the associated health risks of cholesterol.

ATHEROSCLEROSIS

Atherosclerosis, or hardening of the arteries, occurs with a diet high in saturated fats and cholesterol which causes deposits of cholesterol to be laid down on the walls of the blood vessels. This leads to reduced blood flow to various parts of the body, including the heart, causing **coronary heart disease**; the brain, increasing the possibility of a **stroke**; and the legs, causing **aches** and **pains** when walking.

Cholesterol in foods comes only from animal sources as it is a component of the cell walls of animals. The amount in many processed foods depends on the products used in manufacture and this can vary from batch to batch, depending on the cost and availability of the ingredients. Cholesterol is **not** found in any plant foods including fruit, vegetables, cereals and nuts. So if you are trying to reduce your intake of dietary cholesterol it is beneficial to substitute these plant foods for animal products. An added benefit of plant foods is that they are mostly high in fibre and some types of fibre have been shown to assist in reducing blood cholesterol levels.

DAILY CHOLESTEROL INTAKE

- There is a wide individual response to intake of dietary cholesterol, which is probably due to an inherited predisposition.
- The body manufactures up to 80 per cent of its cholesterol, so changing your diet is not always rewarded by a drop in blood cholesterol levels.
- The cholesterol in seafoods is actually in a different form and does not contribute to elevated blood cholesterol levels.
- An accepted recommended safe intake of cholesterol is:
  200–400 mg per day

RECOMMENDED DAILY INTAKE OF FATS

It is suggested that you aim to balance your intake of saturated and unsaturated fats by having ⅓ to ½ of your fat intake as saturated fats and ½ to ⅔ as unsaturated and monounsaturated fats. Remember, saturated fats come from animal sources and unsaturated and monounsaturated fats come from plant sources. Fats should comprise between 10–30 per cent of your daily energy intake.

Daily energy intake	Total fat
4200 kJ (1000 Cals)	14–35 g
5000 kJ (1200 Cals)	15–40 g
6300 kJ (1500 Cals)	18–50 g
7600 kJ (1800 Cals)	20–60 g
8400 kJ (2000 Cals)	25–70 g
10500 kJ (2500 Cals)	30–85 g
12550 kJ (3000 Cals)	35–100 g

FAT AND CHOLESTEROL GUIDE

	Fat g	Chol. mg		Fat g	Chol. mg
BEVERAGES			White, 35 g	0.5	neg.
Beer, 250 ml	0	0	Breakfast cereals, 30 g		
Cocoa powder, 2 tsp,			All bran	1.5	0
10 g	1.5	neg.	Branflakes	0.5	0
Coffee, brewed, 250 g	0	0	Corn flakes	0	0
Cordial, diluted, 200 ml	0	0	Muesli, Swiss style	2.8	0
Fruit juice, 20 ml	0	0	Toasted	5	0
Malted milk powder,			Rice bubbles	0	0
2 tsp, 10 g	1.5	12	Special K	0.5	0
Milo, 2 tsp, 10 g	1.5	28	Cakes, average 1 slice,		
Ovaltine, 2 tsp, 10 g	1.3	10	100 g		
Soft drinks, average,			Chocolate	18	105
250 ml	0	0	Fruit	55	40
Wine, average, 120 ml	0	0	Sponge	46	73
			Flour, 1 cup, 100 g		
CEREALS			Corn	0.5	0
Biscuits, 1 average,			Plain	1.2	0
25 g			Self-raising	1.2	0
Chocolate coated	6	4	Soya, full fat	24	13
Cream	6	6	Low fat	7	4
Chocolate coated	7	3.5	Wholemeal	2	0
Crispbread	neg.	neg.	Pancakes, 75 g	10	44
Dry cracker	5	1.5			
Fruit filled	2.5	3	**EGGS**		
High fat cracker	5	2	Egg, raw, boiled,		
Sweet	5	5	poached, 55 g	5.5	206
Bread, 1 slice,			Scrambled with milk,		
wholemeal or			100 g	13.5	173
brown, 25 g	0.5	0	Egg white	0	0
1 slice, white, 25 g	0.5	0	Omelette, 2 eggs with		
Garlic bread, 2 slices,			30 g cheese	21	443
50 g	9	6	Quiche Lorraine, 100 g	42	195
Pita, 25 g	0.5	0			
Roll, wholemeal or					
brown, 35 g	0.5	neg.			

	g	mg
FATS, OILS, BUTTER, MARGARINE		
Butter, 1 tsp, 5 g	4.5	10
1 tbsp, 20 g	16	40
Margarine, 1 tsp, 5 g	4	0
1 tbsp, 20 g	16	0
Margarine, fat reduced,		
1 tsp, 5 g	2	0
1 tbsp, 20 g	8	0
Copha, 20 g	20	0
Dripping, lard, 20 g	20	17
Oil, all types, 1 tbsp,		
20 ml	20	0
½ cup, 125 ml	125	0
FISH AND SEAFOODS		
Anchovies, 45 g	4.5	35
Crabmeat, 100 g	0.5	84
Fish paste, 30 g	27	19
Gemfish, 100 g	13	80
Mussels, oysters, 1 doz,		
120 g	3	97
Prawns, 6 boiled, 120 g	1	225
Salmon, average,		
canned, 100 g	10	70
Sardines, 1 can, 60 g	9.5	68
Scallops, 10 steamed,		
100 g	1.5	60
Tuna, canned in brine,		
drained, 100 g	2.5	53
Canned in oil,		
drained, 100	13.5	40
Whiting, steamed, 100 g	1	104
FRUIT		
Most fruits have negligible		
amounts of fat and no cholesterol.		
Avocado, ½, 100 g	22.5	0
Olives, 10 medium, 50 g	1.8	0

	g	mg
GRAINS, PULSES, BEANS		
Cannellini beans,		
canned, 100 g	0.5	0
Chickpeas, canned,		
100 g	2	0
Kidney beans, dried,		
100 g	2	0
Lentils, dried, 100 g	2	0
Lima beans, dried,		
100 g	1.5	0
Soya beans, dried,		
100 g	20	0
Split peas, dried, 100 g	2	0
MEAT AND MEAT PRODUCTS		
(raw weight 100 g)		
Beef		
As purchased with fat,		
grilled/baked	13.5	78
All visible fat removed,		
grilled/baked	6.5	75
Lamb		
As purchased with fat,		
grilled/baked	26.5	110
All visible fat removed,		
grilled/baked	8	109
Pork		
As purchased with fat,		
grilled/baked	22	90
All visible fat removed,		
grilled/baked	5	90
Veal		
As purchased with fat,		
grilled/baked	4	110
All visible fat removed,		
grilled/baked	2.5	110

FAT AND CHOLESTEROL GUIDE

Chicken	g	mg
As purchased with fat and skin, grilled/baked	16.5	130
All visible fat and skin removed, grilled/baked	8	130
Offal		
Beef kidney, simmered	2.5	550
Lamb brains, simmered	9.5	1890
Liver, fried	13.5	585
Oxtail, simmered	29	60
Veal kidney, grilled	6.5	435
Liver, grilled	8	245
Sausages		
Beef, grilled/fried, 100 g	18	70
Frankfurter, boiled, 100 g	20	60
Pork, grilled/fried, 100 g	21	60

MILK PRODUCTS
Milk – fresh and UHT
(1 glass, 200 ml)

	g	mg
Whole	7.5	30
Fat reduced	3.5	10
Skim	0.2	8
Goat's	5	18
Human	4	30
Soy	4	0
Evaporated and condensed		
Whole, 30 ml	2.5	6
Skim, 30 ml	0.1	1
Dried and powdered		
Whole, 1 tbsp, 12 g	3	12
Skim, 1 tbsp, 10 g	0.1	3.5
Yoghurt		
(per 200 ml carton)		
Plain, natural	9	28
Non fat, natural	0.5	4

	g	mg
Flavoured	4	16
Non fat, flavoured	0.5	4
Cheeses		
(3 cm cube, 30 g)		
Camembert	8	28
Cheddar	10	30
Cheese spread	7	20
Cottage	3	11
Cream cheese	8.5	27
Danish blue	10	35
Edam	9	23
Parmesan	10	29
Processed	9	25
Ricotta	3	14
Swiss	10	26
Cream		
Pure, 35%, 30 ml	10.5	30
Reduced fat, 25%, 30 ml	8	25
Sour cream, 35%, 30 ml	11	30
Reduced fat, 25%, 30 ml	6	19
Sour cream dip, 30 ml	5	11
Thickened, 35%, 30 ml	11	35

SAUCES, SPREADS, CONDIMENTS
Sauces and condiments

	g	mg
Barbeque, 20 ml	neg.	0
Gravy, 20 ml	3	4.5
Mayonnaise, 20 ml	6.5	6.5
Reduced fat, 20 ml	4	5
Mustard, 5 ml	neg.	0
Salad dressing, 20 ml	5	0
Soy, 20 ml	0	0
Tomato, 20 ml	neg.	0

	g	mg
White, home made, 20 ml	2	4
Worcestershire, 20 ml	neg.	0
Spreads		
Fish paste, 10 g	1	6
Jam, 20 g	0	0
Treacle, 30 g	0	0
Vegemite, 3 g	neg.	0
SEEDS AND NUTS		
Almonds, 12, 20 g	11	0
Brazil nuts, 5, 20 g	14	0
Cashews, 10, 20 g	10	0
Hazel nuts, 13, 20 g	12	0
Macadamia, 9, 20 g	15	0
Peanuts, 25, 20 gm	9.5	0
Pistachio, 30, 20 g	10	0
Sesame seeds, 20 g	11	0
Walnuts, 5, 20 g	14	0
Tahini spread, 50 g	30	0
TAKE-AWAY FOODS		
Chicken		
Chicken nuggets, 6 average	17	70
Kentucky fried, average, 100 g	20	95
Hamburgers		
Plain, 150 g	15.5	39
Bacon, 170 g	22	49
Cheese, 170 g	22	58
Egg, 200 g	24	220
The lot, 300 g	30	250
McDonalds, Big Mac	32	90
Fried Food		
Fish and chips	35	60
Chiko roll, 1 average, 190 g	20	14

	g	mg
Chips, 1 bucket, 150 g	21	18
Dim sims, 1 fried, 50 g	5	4
Potato cake, 1 average, 50 g	11	10
Pasta		
(per 250 g serve)		
Spaghetti, fettuccine etc. with:		
Bolognaise sauce	20	100
Carbonara sauce	27	300
Napolitana sauce	5	neg.
Cannelloni, ricotta filled, tomato sauce	5	5
Meat filled, tomato sauce	10	80
Lasagna	18	95
Ravioli, meat sauce	20	100
Pies and Pasties		
Meat pie, 1 average, 180 g	14	36
Pastie, 1 average, 160 g	20	80
Sausage roll, 1 average, 100 g	18	20
Pizza		
Average, ½ medium pizza, 250 g	25	30
Frozen pizza supreme, 250 g	27	48
Pizza Hut, ham and pineapple, 250 g	21	28
Supreme, 250 g	22	25
Average with extra cheese, 250 g	26	33
VEGETABLES		

All vegetables have low levels of fat and no cholesterol.

VITAMINS, MINERALS AND SALT

Vitamins are organic substances, most of which our bodies cannot manufacture from raw materials. They are involved in virtually every process in the body, so although we need only very small amounts, they are essential. Minerals are inorganic substances which also play an essential role in the body's functioning.

The best way of ensuring you are getting the vitamins and minerals you need is by eating a balanced variety of foods every day and avoiding the energy rich/nutritionally empty foods such as confectionery and processed foods. Vitamin-mineral supplements shouldn't be seen as insurance against the effects of a poor diet, but if you do take added vitamins and minerals, avoid megadosing as too much can be harmful. A vitamin-mineral supplement may be advisable if you are reducing your daily food intake to less than 5000 kilojoules (1200 calories).

SALT

Our typical diets are high in one particular mineral — sodium. This occurs naturally in many foods, but is often added in the form of salt as well as in common food additives such as baking powder, some preservatives and monosodium glutamate (MSG).

HIGH BLOOD PRESSURE

In genetically predisposed individuals, a high intake of sodium is linked with high blood pressure (hypertension). Salt is not necessarily the most important factor causing high blood pressure in all individuals, but the indications are that most people should reduce their intake. Your taste buds take a little time to adjust to less salty foods, but with gradual reductions you won't notice the difference. Try to add less or no salt to your foods and avoid the processed and take-away foods that are high in salt. A list of foods and their sodium content follows.

RECOMMENDED SAFE AND ADEQUATE SODIUM INTAKE PER DAY

	milligrams
Adults	900–2300
Infants	100–600
Children	300–2300

SODIUM GUIDE

BEVERAGES

	Sodium mg
Cocoa powder, 10 g	95
Cordial, prepared, 1 glass, 200 ml	20
Drinking chocolate, 10 g	25
Milo, 10 g	50
Mineral water, natural, 1 glass, 200 ml	16
With juice	30
Ovaltine, 10 g	25
Soft drinks, 1 glass, 200 ml	28

CEREALS

	mg
Biscuit, chocolate, 1 average	32
gingernut, 1 average	22
Breads, average slice	125
Breakfast cereals, ½ cup, 30 g	
Corn flakes	351
Rice bubbles	318
Weeties	155
Cakes, 1 slice, 50 g	
Chocolate	250
Fruit	175
Plain, vanilla	275
Flour, 1 cup, 100 g	
Gravy powder	8200
Plain	2
Self-raising	695
Pastry, 100 g	480

EGGS

	mg
Egg, 55 g	77
Scrambled, with milk, 100 g	140

FISH

	mg
Anchovies, oil drained, 30 g	1644
Crab, 100 g	400
Fresh fish, average, 100 g	100
Oysters, 12 g	612
Prawns, 100 g	1590
Salmon, canned, 100 g	570
Sardines, canned, 100 g	540
Tuna, canned, 100 g	420

FRUIT

All fresh fruits have negligible sodium

	mg
Dried fruits, average, 30 g	24
Olives in brine, 5, 20 g	360

MEAT AND MEAT PRODUCTS (per 100 g)

	mg
Bacon	1870
Beef, average, most cuts	55
Corned	1200
Chicken, average	70
Duck, average	70
Lamb, average, most cuts	60
Rolled, seasoned	220
Pork, average, most cuts	50
Veal, average, most cuts	80
Processed meats	
Frankfurter	980
Liverwurst	860
Luncheon meat, canned	1050
Salami	1850
Sausages	1090
Tongue, canned	1050

MILK PRODUCTS	mg
Milk — fresh and UHT **(1 glass, 200 ml)**	
Whole	100
Fat reduced	100
Skim	100
High protein skim	100
Goat's	80
Human	20
Flavoured	100
Evaporated and condensed	
Condensed, 2 tbsp, 50 g	90
Evaporated, 2 tbsp, 30 g	54
Dried and powdered	
Whole, 1 tbsp, 12 g	53
Skim, 1 tbsp, 10 g	55
Yoghurt **(per 200 ml carton)**	
Plain, natural	80
Non-fat, natural	150
Flavoured	80
Non-fat, flavoured	128
Cheeses **(3 cm cube, 30 g)**	
Average cheese dips	200
Camembert	425
Cheddar	183
Cheese spread	350
Cottage	135
Cream cheese	90
Danish blue	425
Edam	295
Parmesan	225
Processed	410
Ricotta	60
Swiss	47

Cream	mg
Average, 100 ml	60

SPREADS, SAUCES, CONDIMENTS	
Barbeque sauce, 10 ml	82
Chutney, 1 tbsp, 10 g	12
Fish paste, 5 g	30
Honey, jam, average, 20 g	2
Mayonnaise, 20 g	72
Meat paste, 5 g	37
Pickles, mustard, 20 g	240
Peanut butter, 20 g	105
Salad dressing, 20 ml	195
Soy sauce, 10 ml	733
Stock cubes, 10 g	1030
Table salt, ½ tsp, 1 g	390
Tartare sauce, 20 ml	140
Tomato sauce, 20 ml	70
Vegemite, 5 g	208

SEEDS AND NUTS	
Plain nuts, average, 20 g	1
Roast, salted, average, 20 g	48

SOUPS	
Average, tinned or packet, 200 ml	650

SNACK FOODS AND CONFECTIONERY	
Boiled sweets, 50 g	35
Bounty bar, 50 g	65
Caramels, 50 g	125
Carob bar, 50 g	40
Chocolate, milk, 50 g	45
Milk, filled or with nuts, 50 g	38
Dark, 50 g	27
Corn chips, plain, 50 g	175
Flavoured, 50 g	255

	mg
Extruded cheese products e.g. Twisties, Cheezels, Burger rings, 50 g	550
Fruit and honey bar, 50 g	23
Licorice, 50 g	60
Mars bar, 50 g	80
Muesli bars, 1 average, fruit, 30 g	15
Choc. coated, choc. chip, 30 g	75
Popcorn, unsalted, 50 g	neg.
Salted, 50 g	490
Potato crisps, flavoured, 50 g	320
Sesame bar, 50 g	15
Violet crumble, 50 g	130

TAKE-AWAY FOODS

Chiko roll, 100 g	350
Dim sim, fried, 50 g	535
Garlic bread, 50 g	190
Hamburger, plain, 200 g	1320
With bacon, 200 g	1560
With cheese, 200 g	1520
McDonalds, big Mac, 200 g	1140
Cheeseburger	820
Fillet o' Fish	900
Hot cakes and syrup	1130
McFeast	950
Quarter pounder with cheese	1410
Sundae	120
Meat pie, 180 g	1080
Pasta, average, 100 g	250
Pizza, average, Pizza Hut, 100 g	700

VEGETABLES
Most fresh vegetables have negligible amounts

Canned vegetables, average, 100 g	250

TEN STEPS FOR REDUCING SODIUM

1 Don't add any salt to your food at the table — throw out the salt shaker!

2 Add very little or no salt when cooking.

3 Cut down on your salt intake gradually to allow your tastes to adapt to the change.

4 Reduce intake of processed foods as they can contribute up to half of your intake of sodium. Always choose 'salt reduced' alternatives.

5 Reduce your consumption of take-away foods including chips, hamburgers and pizza.

6 Choose Chinese dishes carefully; avoid highly salted dishes and added MSG (Monosodium glutamate).

7 Reduce consumption of mineral waters.

8 Avoid the hidden salt in cakes, pastries, biscuits and sauces.

9 Balance sodium intake with potassium rich foods such as fresh and frozen fruits and vegetables.

10 Rock salt, sea salt and seasoned salt are all salt and should be reduced. Sodium also occurs in baking powder, monosodium glutamate (MSG) and some preservatives.

BABY FOODS

HEINS (per 100 ml/100 g)	kJ	Cals
Strained juices		
Apple juice	195	47
Apple and blackcurrant juice	175	41
Apple and rosehip juice	185	44
Orange and banana juice	145	35
Orange juice	140	34
Prune and apple juice	180	43
Tropical fruit juice	185	43
Cereals		
High protein cereal	1460	349
Mixed cereal	1440	344
Muesli and fruit, per 200 g	1650	394
Rice cereal	1500	358
Strained yoghurt desserts		
Apple	315	75
Apricot	325	78
Banana	330	79
Fruit salad dessert	315	75
Orange	325	78
Passionfruit	355	85
Peach	290	69
Pineapple	280	67
Raspberry	360	86
Strawberry	310	75
Strained gels		
Apple	250	59
Apple and blackcurrant	250	60
Cherry	220	53
Fruit salad	290	70

	kJ	Cals
Orange	255	61
Rosehip	220	52
Kiwi fruit	285	68
Tropical fruits	270	65
Strained savoury		
Beef and vegetables	310	74
Brains	230	55
Chicken and noodles	225	53
Chicken and vegetables	230	54
Chicken broth	235	55
Creamed chicken	270	64
Egg yolk and steak	270	65
Lamb and vegetables	255	61
Mixed vegetables	185	44
Steak and vegetables	260	63
Turkey and vegetables	240	57
Strained desserts		
Apples	215	52
Apricots and rice	285	68
Banana custard	315	75
Caramel custard	330	79
Chocolate custard	265	64
Egg custard	285	68
Fruit custard	310	74
Peach and apple	240	58
Tropical fruit	285	68
Junior savoury		
Beef dinner	275	66
Chicken and vegetables	265	63
Chicken dinner	215	51
Egg and steak	250	60
Lamb dinner	255	61
Steak and vegetables	305	72

BEVERAGES

ALCOHOLIC DRINKS

Beer

DRAUGHT/LAGER

Average (4.7% alcohol)	kJ	Cals
140 ml	205	50
200 ml	295	70
285 ml	420	100
375 ml, 1 can or stubbie	555	133
750 ml, 1 bottle	1105	265

LOW ALCOHOL

Average (2.2% alcohol)		
140 ml	145	35
200 ml	210	50
285 ml	300	72
375 ml, 1 can or stubbie	395	95
750 ml, 1 bottle	790	190

STOUT

Average (7% alcohol)		
140 ml	280	67
200 ml	400	95
285 ml	570	135
750 ml, 1 bottle	1500	360

SHANDY

Beer/Lemonade 1:1		
200 ml	325	80
285 ml	465	110
Beer/Low joule lemonade 1:1		
200 ml	150	35
285 ml	215	50

Brand Names

CARLTON AND UNITED BREWERIES (per 375 ml)	kJ	Cals
Abbots double stout	750	180
Abbots invalid stout	710	170
Carlton D-ale	470	115
Carlton genuine draught	580	140
Carlton light	470	115
Carlton special light	265	65
Export light	205	45
Foster's lager	600	145
Foster's light	395	95
KB lager	560	135
Kent old brown	545	130
Reschs DA	580	140
Reschs draught	545	130
Reschs pilsener	545	130
Sheaf stout	790	190
Victoria bitter	600	145

CASCADE (per 375 ml)		
2.7% Light	375	90
Bitter	565	135
Pale Ale	585	140
Premium Lager	630	150

CASTLEMAINE (per 375 ml)		
XXXX bitter ale	610	135
XXXX gold	415	100
XXXX light bitter	370	90
XXXX original draught	570	135
Carbine stout	725	170

Castlemaine	kJ	Cals
Special dry	550	130
Castlemaine 2.2	350	80
DL lager	460	110

COOPERS
(per 375 ml)

	kJ	Cals
Light beer	340	80
Draught beer	490	115
Sparkling ale	640	150
Pale ale	525	125
Stout	790	190
Birell (brewed soft drink)	300	70

SOUTH AUSTRALIAN BREWING CO.
(per 375 ml)

	kJ	Cals
Best bitter	550	130
Broken Hill draught	595	145
Kent Town ale	650	155
Southwark bitter	575	135
Southwark gold	475	115
Southwark lite	350	85
Southwark premium	680	165
Southwark special	455	110
Old **Southwark** stout	880	210
West End draught	550	130
West End export	595	145
West End extra light	220	55
West End light	370	90
West End super	610	145

TOOHEY'S
(per 375 ml)

	kJ	Cals
Blue	550	130
Country	505	120
Draft	590	140
Dry	610	145
Lite 2.2%	375	90
Old	580	140
Red	640	150

WESTERN AUSTRALIAN BEERS
(per 375 ml)

	kJ	Cals
Swan stout	910	220
Swan dry	600	145
Swan lager	625	150
Swan draught	605	145
Swan export	605	145
Swan gold	445	110
Swan special	290	70
Emu export	625	150
Emu bitter	580	140
Emu club lager	400	95
Hannan's lager	535	130

Cider

(average, 1 glass, 200 ml)

Dry cider	330	80
Draught cider	360	85
Sweet cider	420	100
Sweet non-alcoholic cider	420	100

Cocktails and Mixed Drinks

(per 1 glass 200 ml)

Bloody Mary (vodka and tomato juice)	455	110
Bourbon/rum/brandy and cola	560	135
Brandy and dry ginger	455	110
Gin and bitter lemon	610	145
Gin and tonic	535	128
Lemon/lime and bitters	400	95
Screwdriver (vodka and orange)	522	125

(per 100 ml)	kJ	Cals
Brandy Alexander/ Grasshopper	780	187
Daiquiri	800	190
Margarita	550	130
Martini	450	110
Whisky sour	690	165

Drink Additives

	kJ	Cals
Angostura bitters	negligible	
Claytons, 30 ml	560	135

Liqueurs

(per liqueur glass, 30 ml)	kJ	Cals
Apricot/peach brandy, kirsch, malibu	250	60
Advocaat, cassis, calvados, cherry brandy	315	75
Creme de menthe, galliano, grand marnier, tia maria	375	90
Bailey's Irish cream, Benedictine, Cointreau, Drambuie, kahlua	425	100
Chartreuse	500	120

Spirits

	kJ	Cals
Average, ½ nip, 15 ml	130	30
1 nip, 30 ml	260	60
1 jigger, 60 ml	520	120
½ bottle, 375 ml	3195	765
Brandy, 1 nip, 30 ml	257	60

	kJ	Cals
Gin, whisky, bourbon, 1 nip, 30 ml	269	64
Rum, vodka, 1 nip, 30 ml	267	63

Wines

(120 ml = 1 wine glass)
(60 ml = 1 port/sherry glass)

	kJ	Cals
Champagne, dry, average, 120 ml	325	77
With orange, 1:1, 120 ml	290	70
Madeira, average, 60 ml	375	89
Marsala, average, 60 ml	120	30
Port, average, 60 ml	375	90
Red, dry (shiraz, cabernet, chianti, rose), 120 ml	340	80
Sparkling (lambrusco, cold duck), 120 ml	380	90
Sherry, dry, average, 60 ml	260	60
Sweet/cream, average, 60 ml	355	85
Vermouth, dry, 60 ml	295	71
Sweet, 60 ml	350	83
White, dry (semillon, riesling, chardonnay), 120 ml	340	80
Sweet (moselle, fruity lexia), 120 ml	385	92
Wine coolers, 3–4% alcohol, average 120 ml	265	63

Non-Alcoholic Wines

CHATEAU YALDARA (per 100 ml)	kJ	Cals
Grapella — red	660	158
Grapella — white	660	158
Lambrusco	540	129
Riesling	285	68
Spumante	540	129

COOPER'S (per 100 ml)		
Birell	80	19

ORLANDO (per 100 ml)		
Maison spumante	135	33
Maison supreme white	185	45
Peach maison	220	53
Rosé maison	220	53
White maison	185	45

Wine Coolers

(per 120 ml)		
Average, 3–4% alcohol	265	63

ORLANDO		
Tropical cooler	285	68
Wild lime cooler	290	69
Wild mango cooler	350	83
Wild peach cooler	270	65

BONOX, BOVRIL, HORLICKS

	kJ	Cals
Bonox/Bovril, 1 tsp, 4 g	40	10
Horlicks, 1 tbsp, 10 g	160	40

COFFEE

	kJ	Cals
Instant: Black, 1 tsp, 5 g powder	20	5
White, 2 tsp milk	50	11
White, 1 tbsp milk	75	18
White, 1½ tbsp milk	105	25
White, 1 tbsp skim milk	50	12
Decaffeinated: See Instant		
Espresso, dripolated: See Instant		
Cappuccino	300	72
Vienna, with 1 tbsp cream	240	57
Jarrah international: Swiss mocha, cafe au lait, coffee & cinnamon, per tbsp, 20 g	400	95
No caffeine coffee substitutes: caro, ecco etc, 1 heaped tsp, 2 g	25	6
Coffee whitener, 1 heaped tsp, 8 g	170	40
For each teaspoon of sugar add	65	16

CORDIALS

20 ml = 1 tbsp 200 ml = 1 glass	kJ	Cals
Average, undiluted,		
20 ml	160	40
Diluted 1:4, 200 ml	400	95
Citrus 25% juice,		
undiluted, 20 ml	140	35
Diluted 1:4, 200 ml	350	85
Citrus 60% juice,		
undiluted, 20 ml	160	40
Diluted 1:4, 200 ml	400	95
Lemon, undiluted, 20 ml	180	45
Diluted 1:4, 200 ml	450	110
Lemon barley, undiluted,		
20 ml	170	40
Diluted 1:4, 200 ml	425	100
Lime, undiluted, 20 ml	160	40
Diluted 1:4, 200 ml	400	95
Orange, undiluted, 20 ml	150	35
Diluted 1:4, 200 ml	375	90
Low joule average,		
undiluted, 20 ml	15	5
Diluted, 1:4, 200 ml	40	10

Blackcurrant Cordials

	kJ	Cals
Average, undiluted,		
20 ml	170	40
Diluted 1:4, 200 ml	400	95
Berrivale 25%,		
undiluted, 20 ml	110	25
Diluted 1:4, 200 ml	275	65
Ribena, undiluted, 20 ml	240	55
Diluted 1:4, 200 ml	600	145
Tetra-pak, 250 ml	585	140
Blackcurrant and apple,		
undiluted, 20 ml	130	30
Diluted 1:4, 200 ml	320	80

Rose Hip Syrup

	kJ	Cals
Average, undiluted,		
20 ml	200	50
Diluted 1:4, 200 ml	500	120
Unsweetened, undiluted,		
20 ml	65	15
Diluted 1:4, 200 ml	165	40

ENERGY AND ANTACID DRINKS

	kJ	Cals
Eno/Dexsal, 2 tsp, 10 g	15	5
Saline, 2 tsp, 10 g	100	25
Horlicks, 1 tbsp, 20 g	325	80
Lucozade, 1 glass, 200 ml	620	150
Sustagen, 1 carton, 250 ml	1170	280

FRUIT DRINKS AND JUICES

Fruit Drinks (25% juice) (per glass, 200 ml)

	kJ	Cals
Apple	340	80
Orange and mango	320	80
Orange	325	80
Tropical	310	75

Fruit Juice Drinks (5% juice) (per glass, 200 ml)

	kJ	Cals
Apricot juice drink	460	110
Orange and mango drink	450	110
Orange drink	410	100

Fruit Juices (100% juice) (per glass, 200 ml)	kJ	Cals
Average, sweetened	400	95
Unsweetened	300	70
Apple juice, sweetened	390	95
No added sugar	350	85
Carbonated	350	85
Apricot nectar	535	130
Grape juice	470	110
Grapefruit juice, sweetened	380	90
No added sugar	250	60
Lemon juice, sweetened	380	90
No added sugar	280	70
Lime juice, sweetened	350	85
No added sugar	240	60
Mango nectar	485	115
Orange and mango	295	70
Orange, sweetened	300	70
No added sugar	285	70
Freshly squeezed	370	90
Orange and mango, sweetened	300	70
No added sugar	285	70
Peach nectar	545	130
Pineapple juice, canned, sweetened	420	100
No added sugar	390	95
Prune nectar	670	160

Brand Names

BERRI, BIGO, GLENPAK, PATRA, SUNPAK

Long Life/Tetra, Unsweetened (per 100 ml)	kJ	Cals
Apple	170	40
Apple/peach	175	42
Apple/pear	180	43
Dark grape	235	56
Exotic fruit juice	185	45
Grapefruit	140	35
Orange	155	37
Orange, sweetened	170	40
Orange/mango	155	37
Orange/passionfruit	155	37
Pineapple	175	42
Pineapple/mango	175	42
Pineapple/orange	170	40
Tropical	185	45

BREAK

Fruit Drinks (25%) (per 250 ml)		
Apple/blackcurrant	465	111
Apple/cherry	460	110
Apple/raspberry	430	102
Apple/strawberry	450	107
Apple/tropic	450	107
Orange	430	102
Orange/mango	445	105
Tropical	460	110

ORCHY

(per 100 ml)		
Apple juice, unsweetened	185	45

	kJ	Cals
Apple and pineapple juice, long-life	190	45
Lemon-lime sport drink	110	25
Pineapple juice, unsweetened	200	50
Orange juice, unsweetened	185	45

PRIMA
(per 250 ml Tetra-pak)
Fruit Drink (25%)

	kJ	Cals
Apple and mango	445	106
Mandarin/peach	480	115
Orange	445	106
Orange/mango	445	106
Orange/passionfruit	445	106
Tropical	450	108

Fruit Drink (40%)

	kJ	Cals
Apple	445	106
Pineapple	450	108

Fruit Juice (100%)
(unsweetened)

	kJ	Cals
Apple	440	105
Apple/blackcurrant	480	115
Apple/peach	475	113
Apple/tropical	455	109
Orange	395	94
Orange 'premium'	505	120
Orange/mango	400	96
Pineapple/orange	440	105
Tropical	475	114

SCHWEPPES
Juices
(per 100 ml)

	kJ	Cals
Apple	190	45
Apple and blackcurrant	190	45
Apricot nectar fruit juice drink	210	50

	kJ	Cals
Orange	165	40
Orange and mango	160	38
Pineapple	210	50
Tropical fruit juice	185	45

SPRING VALLEY
Fruit Juices
(per 250 ml)

	kJ	Cals
Apple	400	95
Apple and blackcurrant	460	110
Apple and cherry	460	110
Apple and raspberry	490	120
Grapefruit	335	80
Lemon	310	75
Orange	385	90
Orange and mango	400	95
Peach nectar	500	120
Pear nectar	475	115
Pineapple	475	115
Tomato	250	60
Tropical	450	107

Sparkling Juices
(per 300 ml)

	kJ	Cals
Apple	580	140
Cherry	580	140
Lemon	560	135
Orange	580	140

SUNBURST
Juices
(per glass, 250 ml)

	kJ	Cals
Apple, unsweetened, 100%	500	120
Grapefruit, unsweetened	390	93
Orange	450	107
Unsweetened, 100%	390	93
Orange/mango	500	120
Pineapple, unsweetened	485	116

	kJ	Cals
Pineapple crush	545	130
Pineapple/orange	535	128
Fruit Drinks (25%)		
Apple/wildberry	450	107
Mandarin/peach	480	115
Orange	440	105
Orange/mango	450	107
Orange/passionfruit	440	105
Pineapple/coconut	480	115
Tropical	450	107

SOFT DRINKS

(Average, all types)	(200 ml glass)	
Cola	350	83
Bitter lemon	400	95
Dry ginger	230	55
Ginger beer	370	90
Lemon	400	95
Lemonade	350	83
Orange	445	105
Soda water	0	0
Tonic water	310	75

MINERAL WATER

Plain/natural, average	0	0
With fruit juice, average	320	76

DIET SOFT DRINKS

Diet cola, average	2	½
Diet lemonade, average	6	1
Diet dry ginger ale, average	8	2
Diet coke	4	1
Diet pepsi	2	½
Diet Leed lemonade	6	1

	kJ	Cals
Diet sprite	9	2
Just one, all flavours	2	½
Tab	4	1

Brand Names

KOALA SPRINGS

(10% fruit juice)	(285 ml)	
Kiwi, lime and grapefruit	400	95
Lemon, lime and orange	415	99
Mandarin and orange	415	99
Orange and passionfruit	440	105
Raspberry, guava and apple	425	101

SCHWEPPES

Soft Drinks	(375 ml)	
Bitter lemon	725	173
Cola	675	160
Creamy soda	675	160
Dry ginger ale	460	110
Ginger beer	485	115
Lemon, lime, bitter and soda	645	155
Lemon/lime drink	575	137
Lemonade	700	167
Lime flavour	715	170
Pashene	715	170
Plantation pine	685	165
Red creaming soda	735	175
Sarsaparilla	705	168
Soda water	0	0
Solo	740	176
Sunkist orange crush	815	195
Sunshine pine	685	165
Tonic water	575	137

BEVERAGES

	kJ	Cals
Wild raspberry flavour	630	150
Zapple	805	193
Low Joule Diet		
Diet sunkist	45	10
Diet lemonade	20	4
Diet solo	30	7
Low joule cola	5	2
Low joule dry ginger ale	20	4
Low joule tonic water	35	8
Flavoured Mineral Water		
Apple/blackcurrant	780	187
Lemon	755	180
Lemon/lime	595	143
Lemonade	655	157
Lime	550	132
Orange	620	150
Orange/mango	790	189
Orange/passionfruit	570	136
Peach/apple	650	155
Portello	720	172

WEIGHT WATCHERS	**(375 ml)**	
Low joule lemonade	15	4
Flavoured Mineral Water		
Lemon	20	5
Orange	40	10
Orange and mango	45	11

TEA

(average, all brewing methods)		
Black, 250 ml	10	2
White, 2 tsp milk	35	9
1 tbsp milk	65	15
1½ tbsp milk	90	22
1 tbsp skim milk	40	9

VEGETABLE JUICES

(per glass, 200 ml)	kJ	Cals
Tomato, canned, average,		
sweetened, 200 ml	220	50
Unsweetened, 200 ml	190	45
Vegetable, canned,		
average, 200 ml	220	55
Homemade — calculate from		
kilojoules of vegetables used.		

Brand Names

HEINZ
(per 100 ml)

Tomato juice	105	25
Unsweetened	90	21

LETONA
(per 100 ml)

Tomato juice,		
sweetened	75	18
Unsweetened	60	15

BEVERAGES

CANNED, FROZEN AND PACKET MEALS

CANNED MEALS

(per 100 g)	kJ	Cals
EDGELL		
Asparagus turkey	415	98
Baked beans	345	82
Curried	345	82
Beef ravioli	365	87
Stroganoff	475	115
Casserole provençale	305	73
Cheese and spinach		
ravioli	259	62
Chicken ravioli	410	97
Tortellini	405	97
Chilli beef and beans	405	96
Chinese satay	270	65
Classic cacciatore	240	57
Hot pots, farmhouse	410	100
Italian	275	65
Mexican beef and pasta	480	115
Oriental sweet and sour	390	93
Penne bolognaise	380	91
Spaghetti	275	65
Curried	275	65

HARVEST		
(per serve, ½ can, 212 g)		
Irish stew	550	131
Mornay chicken	555	132
Sweet curry	540	129
Sweet and sour pork	630	150
Vegetables and		
sausages	545	130
Vegetables and steak	490	117

HEINZ (per 100 g)	kJ	Cals
Alphaghetti in tomato		
sauce	275	66
Spaghetti, bolognaise	240	57
Invaders shapes in		
tomato sauce	295	71
Oops tomato sauce		
and cheese	275	66
Salt reduced in		
tomato sauce	255	61
Spooky shapes in		
tomato sauce	275	66
Tomato sauce and		
cheese	255	61
Wholemeal	275	66
Super snacks		
Bolognaise, ravioli	350	84
Spaghetti	360	83
Tortellini	395	94
Rice and beef curry	505	121
Vegetable beef		
casserole	450	108
Kids cuisine		
Curried rice and steak	375	83
Farmhouse chicken		
casserole	340	81
Macaroni steak dinner	330	79
Pasta and chicken		
supreme	410	97
Rice, steak and onions	350	83
Savoury rice with beef	340	81
Spaghetti bolognaise	280	67
Curried in tomato		
sauce	240	58

	kJ	Cals
Tomato sauce and cheese	230	54
Vegetables, spring lamb hotpot	315	75
And steak	365	87

KRAFT
(per serve, ½ can, 220 g)

	kJ	Cals
Beef steak and mushroom	1230	295
Steak and vegetables	1740	416
Stroganoff	1475	352
Sweet curry	1475	352
Braised steak and onions	1520	363
Snack size	760	182
Irish stew	750	179
Ravioli	1080	258
Spaghetti bolognaise	835	199
With meatballs	915	218
Vegetables and sausages	850	203

SANITARIUM (per 100 g)

	kJ	Cals
B-B-Q links	760	62
Bologna	840	55
Casserole mince	320	80
Nutmeat	740	60
Nutolene	920	60
Salad loaf	480	72
Savoury pie	720	63
Soya loaf	760	56
Swiss rounds	640	65
Tender bits	340	79
Vegecuts	420	73
Vegelinks	700	65
Vegetarian country stew	320	82
Vegetarian rediburger	680	58
Vegetarian sausages	680	65

FROZEN MEALS

BARON'S TABLE
(per average portion)

	kJ	Cals
Crumbed chicken Kiev, 175 g	1915	458
Chicken schnitzel, 150 g	1615	386
Veal cordon bleu, 140 g	1530	366
Veal schnitzel, 150 g	1565	374

BIRDS EYE (per 100 g)

	kJ	Cals
Crumbed beefburgers	1040	248
Hamburgers	1030	245
Microwiz, cheeseburgers	1075	256
Hamburgers	1070	255
Pasta, curry vegetable	520	124
Italian vegetable	445	106
Mexican vegetable	490	116
Sandwich steaks	1050	250
Veal schnitzels	1015	242

FINDUS
Lean cuisine (per meal)

	kJ	Cals
Beef, italienne	1070	255
Oriental	1090	260
Cheese cannelloni	1065	255
Chicken, breast of, marsala	815	195
Coconut	1045	250
Glazed	1025	242
Lasagna, tuna	1130	270
Traditional	1065	255
Zucchini	1090	260
Macaroni bolognaise	1090	260
Mild vegetable curry	1045	250
Pasta marinara	980	234

	kJ	Cals
Seafood gratin	1065	255
Spaghetti with beef and mushroom sauce	1255	300
Turkey breast with tagliatelle	1110	265
Turkey Dijon	1210	290
Findus Meals (per meal)		
Beef teriyaki	1690	404
Cannelloni	1400	334
Chicken and broccoli	1365	326
Chicken and pasta	1430	342
Fettucini Alfredo	2600	621
Lasagna, bechamel	1870	447
Bolognaise	1665	397
Macaroni and beef	2315	553
Mongolian lamb	1150	275
Sliced beef and capsicum	1690	404
Spaghetti bolognaise	1205	288
Sweet and sour pork	1200	287
Tuna noodle gratin	1590	389
GRIFFS (400 g serve)		
Beef, and black bean sauce	1825	436
Casserole	1755	419
Mild curry	1870	447
Chicken, green Thai curry, 350 g	1930	461
Korma	2090	500
Lemon	1875	448
Mexicana	1625	388
Mornay	1990	476
Red Thai curry, 350 g	1845	441
Curried prawns	1240	296
Lasagne, bolognaise	3065	733
Vegetable	1930	461

	kJ	Cals
Ravioli bolognaise	4385	1049
Red lamb curry	2270	543
Rice, fried, 350 g	2360	564
Hawaiian, 350 g	3605	862
Spinach and lamb curry	2160	516
Sweet and sour pork	2045	489
Tortellini boscaiola	2720	650
INGHAMS (per average portion)		
Chicken breasts in Italian sauce, 175 g	895	214
Mini drums in barbecue sauce, 100 g	720	172
Mini roasts, gravy and seasoning, 200 g	1310	313
Roll, 100 g	890	213
Tenderloins in satay sauce, 175 g	1080	258
Crumbed chicken big dippers, 10 g	145	35
Breast patties, 85 g	1010	241
Breast tenders, 50 g	525	125
Cordon bleu, 100 g	890	213
Drumsticks, 100 g	1070	256
Duets (ham and cheese), 150 g	1350	323
Fillets, 100 g	1045	250
Kiev, 100 g	1020	244
Mini drums, 100 g	1270	303
Nuggets, 20 g	270	65
Parmigiana, 175 g	1270	303
Honey roasted chicken Drumsticks, 100 g	715	171
Mid wings, 100 g	1035	247

McCAINS	kJ	Cals
Budget gourmet dinners (per dinner)		
Beef hotpot, 400 g		
Beef teriyaki, 300 g	1285	307
Fried rice, 350 g	2220	531
Lasagne, 400 g	2590	619
Macaroni cheese, 400 g	2380	569
Mild lamb curry, 400 g		
Prawn curry, 350 g	1325	316
Shepherds pie, 400 g	1950	466
Spaghetti bolognaise, 400 g	2255	539
Sweet and sour pork, 300 g	1470	351
Traditional dinners		
Pork rib fingers, 310 g	1790	428
Roast, beef, 320 g	1180	282
Chicken, 320 g	1470	351
Lamb, 320 g	1210	289
Pork, 320 g	1190	284
Turkey, 320 g	1320	315
Steak Dianne, 320 g	1415	338
Veal parmigiana, 320 g	1755	419
Healthy choice dinners (per dinner)		
Fillet of, lamb, 310 g	1050	251
Veal, 310 g	1230	294
Glazed chicken, 300 g	1230	294
Looney tunes dinners (per dinner)		
Bugs Bunny chicken nuggets, 200 g	1310	313
Daffy Duck spaghetti bolognaise, 200 g	1340	320
Sylvester fish fingers, 200 g	1110	265
Tweety macaroni and cheese, 200 g	1590	380

Pizzas

(per 100 g, ⅕ approx)	kJ	Cals
BIRDS EYE		
Microwiz ham and pineapple	900	215
Supreme	880	210
McCAINS (per 100 g)		
Cheese and bacon	980	235
Ham and pineapple	915	218
Supreme		
Microwave, ham and pineapple	775	185
Pepperoni supremo	870	208
Supreme	845	202
Pizza slice, ham and pineapple, 600 g	5390	1289
Supreme, 600 g	5220	1248
Singles, ham and pineapple	835	199
Supreme	865	206
Subs, ham and pineapple	1385	331
Supreme	1450	346
Turtle microwave, cheese and bacon, 250 g	2655	635
Double cheese, 250 g	2580	617
PAPA GIUSEPPE		
Cheese and bacon	900	215
Ham and pineapple	870	208
Supreme	860	206
Pizza-for-one, cheese and bacon	930	222
Ham and pineapple	885	211
Supreme	955	228

	kJ	Cals
Microwave pizza, ham and pineapple	860	205
Supreme	910	217

Quiches

MAGGI
(per 100 g, ⅕ quiche)

	kJ	Cals
Florentine	1130	270
Lorraine	1385	331
Single serve	1250	299

SARA LEE
(per 100 g, ⅕ quiche)

	kJ	Cals
Lorraine	1115	266
Vegetable	980	234
Light quiches		
Ham, tomato, fetta	665	159
Spinach and ricotta	645	154

Savoury Pastries

(per individual pastry)

FOUR 'N' TWENTY

	kJ	Cals
Pasties, D-Shaped	1835	438
Party	460	110
Pies, chicken	1630	389
Curry and rice	1900	454
Meat	1940	464
Mexicana	1820	435
Party	515	123
Steak and onion	1870	447
Steak and mushroom	1655	395
Sausage rolls, jumbo	1345	321
Large	905	216
Party	465	111

	kJ	Cals
NANNA'S		
Rolls, asparagus mornay, 30 g	290	69
Chiko, 170 g	1115	266
Curry vegetable, 30 g	315	75
Savoury supreme, 30 g	300	71
Sausage, 30 g	285	68
PAMPAS		
(per 100 g)		
Pies, beefsteak	970	232
Chicken and vegetable	880	210
Shepherds	675	161
Single serve	690	165
WEDGWOOD		
Beef croquette	430	102
Pies, chicken	1545	369
Meat	1855	443
Savoury nibbles	120	28
Sausage roll, jumbo	1345	321
Party	505	120
Steak and onion	1835	438
Vol-au-vents (per serve), asparagus	175	41
Chicken	215	51
Chicken and spinach	195	46
Corn	200	47
Egg and bacon	240	57
Hawaiian	230	55
Mexicana	230	55
Mushroom	190	45

See also **Frozen Fish Dinners** on page 90.

PACKET MEALS

CONTINENTAL	kJ	Cals
(per serve, prepared)		
Cookbook casseroles		
Apricot chicken curry	2320	555
Chicken, cacciatore	1415	339
Chasseur	2205	527
Beef, goulash	1005	241
Stroganoff	830	198
Mexican mince	1565	374
Pork in plum	940	225
Sweet and sour	2320	555
Tuna Hollandaise	1870	447
Micro-chef range		
Pasta break, cheddar	1265	302
Creamy mushroom	1315	314
Italiano	1120	268
Pasta perfecto		
Carbonara	760	182
Napolitana	715	170
Romano	740	177
Sicilian mushroom	670	160
Pasta and sauce		
Alfredo	690	165
Chicken curry	660	158
Creamy bacon		
carbonara	680	162
Fettucini verdi	325	77
Mushroom and wine	640	160
Pumpkin with whitemeal		
pasta	480	114
Sour cream and chives	640	155
Mushroom	630	150
Tomato and onion	600	145

	kJ	Cals
MAGGI		
Cook-in-the-pot (per ¼ pack)		
Beef, Bavarian	1025	245
Goulash	1170	279
Oriental	2160	516
Stroganoff	1050	251
Chicken, chasseur	1595	381
In wine	1660	396
Chilli con carne	2215	530
Lamb, Mongolian	2175	520
Ragout	1915	458
Madras curry	855	204
Pasta, bacon and		
mushroom	2910	695
Carbonara	2935	702
Marinara	1735	415
Napolitana	1450	346
Tuna and mushroom	2735	653
WHITE WINGS		
Pasta plus		
(per serve, 4 serves per packet)		
Alfredo	755	180
Boscaiola	765	182
Carbonara	1600	382
Cheese and herb	515	123
Cheese and tomato	510	122
Chicken indiana	515	123
Chicken mushroom	500	119
Mexican chilli	705	168
Napolitana	460	110

CEREAL AND CEREAL PRODUCTS

BISCUITS

Sweet Biscuits

(per biscuit)

ARNOTTS	kJ	Cals
Adora cream	110	26
Arno butter shortbread	250	60
Bolero finger	210	50
Butter cookies	120	29
Butternut cookie	200	47
Chocolate chip	140	34
Coconut rings	200	47
Country cream	410	98
Currant luncheon	215	51
Custard cream	305	73
Date bar	265	63
Delta cream	310	74
Full 'o' fruit	150	36
Glengarry shortbread	295	71
Golden oatmeal	230	55
Granita	145	35
With fruit	235	56
Harvest wheat	100	23
Hazelnut cream	330	79
Honey snaps	140	34
Hundreds and thousands	170	41
Iced vo vo	230	55
Kingston	300	71
Lattice	205	49
Marie	120	29
Milk arrowroot	140	33

	kJ	Cals
Monte Carlo	405	97
Morning coffee	105	25
Nice	185	44
Pecan nut	140	33
Raspberry tartlet	230	55
Scotch finger	355	85
Shortbread cream	370	89
Spicy fruit roll	280	67
Teddy bear	340	80
Tina wafer	180	43
Venetian	260	62
Chocolate Biscuits		
Caramel crown	345	83
Cherry crown	415	99
Chip cream	280	67
Fruit and nut	280	67
Gaiety	290	70
Granita	270	64
Jaffa cake	225	54
Mallows	315	75
Mint slice	355	85
Mintina	175	42
Monte milk/dark	270	65
Peanut wafer	290	69
Ricco	285	68
Sonata	270	65
Stiks	50	11
Tee vee snacks	105	25
Tim tams	410	98
PHOENIX		
Argyle shortbread	140	33
Bavarian	275	65

	kJ	Cals
Chocolate chip	205	50
Chocolate cookies	220	53
Chocolate jaffa	255	61
Jam fancies	300	72
Macaroon delights	260	62
Mallows, mighty	335	80
Strawberry	345	82
Marie	180	43
Nursery rhymes	130	31
Rich coconut	245	58
Roundabouts	265	63
Scotch fingers	235	56
Shortbread, Argyle	140	33
Rich	160	38
Snowballs	315	75
Wheaten, chocolate	260	62
Milk chocolate	260	62

Cream Filled

	kJ	Cals
Banquet	370	88
Custard	300	72
Orange	265	63
Shortbreads, chocolate	285	68
Vanilla	275	65

WESTONS

	kJ	Cals
Butter shortbread drops	130	31
Chocolate chip cookies	185	44
Chocolate delight	290	69
Chocolate 'n' nut	155	37
Fruit bars, chocolate	485	116
Honey and malt	155	37
Milk coconut	200	48
Mint cream, chocolate	295	70
Nice	235	56
Rich tea	165	39
Rocky round	430	103
Wagon wheel	860	205
Wheaten, chocolate	260	62

Crispbreads and Savoury Biscuits

ARNOTTS (per biscuit)	kJ	Cals
Barbeque/beef shapes	40	10
Breton	90	22
Cheds	165	39
Cheese snacks	88	21
Clix	65	16
Country cheese	110	26
Cruskits	120	29
Jatz	70	17
Rye cruskits	90	21
Salada, ¼ biscuit, 1 square	60	14
Sao	160	38
Savoury shapes	35	9
Sesame wheat	130	31
Thin captain, plain	102	24
Vita wheat	95	22
Water cracker, original	50	12

NABISCO	kJ	Cals
Chicken in a biscuit	30	7
Crispy bacon	50	11
Dixie drumsticks	40	9
Minizza	70	17
Premium	70	17
Premium lite	55	13
Ritz	70	17
Water crackers, Captains Table	65	15
Wholemeal premium	60	14

CEREAL AND CEREAL PRODUCTS

	kJ	Cals
WESTONS		
Crackerbread	95	23
Wholemeal	85	20
Ryvita	125	30
Brown	125	30
Hi-fibre	120	29
No-added salt	125	30
Sesame, plain	140	33
Dark	145	34

BRANS AND OATS

	kJ	Cals
Bran		
Oat, raw, 1 tbsp, 10 g	105	25
Rice, 1 tbsp, 10 g	180	43
Wheat, unprocessed, 2 tbsp, 10 g	65	16
Lecithin granules, 1 tbsp, 10 g	200	48
Oats/rolled oats, average		
Rolled, ¼ cup, raw, 30 g	465	110
Porridge, ¾ cup, 175 g	465	110
Instant porridge, 30 g	465	110
Wheatgerm, 1 tbsp, 10 g	110	26

BREAD

	kJ	Cals
Bread, average (white, brown, wholemeal, mixed grain)		
1 cm thick slice, 40 g	390	93
6 mm thin slice, 25 g	245	58

	kJ	Cals
Bun (fruit, hot cross), average per bun, 60 g	760	181
Continental fruit loaf, 40 g	420	98
Croutons, 3 tbsp	200	48
Crumpet, regular, each, 55 g	430	103
Wholemeal, each, 55 g	390	94
Croissants, average, each, 60 g	850	203
SARA LEE, all butter	670	160
Ham and cheese	565	135
Wheat and honey	690	165
Flat bread, 1 white/ wholemeal, 90 g	1100	263
French stick, 2 cm slice, 30 g	300	72
Toast, 1 slice fried, 80 g	840	200
Fruit loaf, light, 1 cm slice, 30 g	335	80
Heavy, 1 cm slice, 40 g	475	115
Garlic bread, 1 slice, 40 g	210	50
Grizzini, 1 stick, 10 g	85	20
Mountain bread, 2 sheets, 40 g	485	115
Muffin, English, each, 65 g	545	130
Fruit, each, 65 g	515	123
See also **Muffins**		
Pita/pocket bread, 1 white/ wholemeal 45 g	550	132

	kJ	Cals
Pritikin bread, 1 cm thick slice, 40 g	390	93
Protein enriched diet bread, average, 1 cm slice, 40 g	390	93
Pumpernickel bread, 6 mm slice, 30 g	230	55
Raisin bread, 1 cm slice, 30 g	335	80
Rye bread, dark, 6 mm slice, 30 g	260	62
Light, 6 mm slice, 30 g	300	76
Rolls (white, wholemeal, mixed grain)		
Bagel, 1 average, 85 g	900	215
Cheese roll, 65 g	700	167
Frankfurter roll, 60 g	600	145
Hamburger, lunch roll, 70 g	755	180
Horseshoe roll, 60 g	600	145
Knot, 60 g	600	145
Small dinner roll, 30 g	320	75
Sourdough bread, 40 g	390	93

Brand Names

(per average slice)
BUTTERCUP

	kJ	Cals
Country split, multigrain	255	61
White	265	64
Wholemeal	240	57
Farmers bake	340	81
Fruit 'n' spice, sandwich	260	63
Toast	335	80
Golden bake, multigrain	225	54
White	225	54
Wholemeal	225	54
Gold medal loaf	295	70
Multigrain	290	69
Multigrain, private label	285	67
Toast, private label	325	78
Naturlich	275	66
Taylors wholemeal	470	112
Vogel, standard	300	72
Light	285	68
Toast	380	92
Wholemeal and sesame	380	91
Wholemeal, sesame and grain	305	73
White sandwich	300	72
White sandwich, private label	285	68
White sandwich toast	330	157
Wholemeal	285	68
Wholemeal sandwich, private label	280	66
Wholemeal toast	330	79
Wholemeal toast, private label	320	77

SUNICRUST
(per average slice)

	kJ	Cals
Naturlich wholemeal	277	66
Pritikin wholemeal	280	66
Seven grain	270	65
Vogel's, oat bran	375	90
Wholemeal and grain	355	85
White, sandwich	270	65
Toast	325	78
Wholemeal, sandwich	255	64
Toast	310	77

	kJ	Cals
TIP TOP		
Burgen, mixed grain	330	79
Oat bran and honey	360	86
Traditional rye	330	79
Cottage bake, multigrain	215	52
White	225	54
Wholemeal	240	57
Harvest wholemeal	415	99
Multigrain	280	67
Multigrain, barley	230	55
Toast	340	81
Spicy fruit loaf	360	86
Sunblest	285	68
Toast	345	68
Weight watchers, mixed grain	185	44
White	190	45
White hyfibe	280	67
Wholemeal	265	64
Wholemeal, hyfibe	265	64
Toast	320	77

WEIGHT WATCHERS

	kJ	Cals
Protein increased white	190	45
Wholemeal mixed grain	185	44

Muffins

(per muffin)

	kJ	Cals
SARA LEE, Apple	1035	247
Blueberry	1040	248
Oatbran	920	220
TIP TOP, English	600	144
Spicy fruit	640	153
Multigrain	610	146
Weight Watchers	510	122

	kJ	Cals
WHITE WINGS		
Country style, per 60 g serve		
Apple and sultana	815	195
Banana and oat bran	815	195
Cinnamon and raisin	870	208

BREAKFAST CEREALS

(per 30 g serve)
CEROLA

	kJ	Cals
Apricot toasted muesli	510	121
Toasted muesli	510	121
Light 'n' crunchy	530	126
Natural muesli	475	114
Oat bran muesli	490	117

KELLOGG'S

	kJ	Cals
All-bran	320	76
Fruit 'n' oats	380	90
Balance oat bran	500	119
With fruit	490	116
Bran flakes	370	88
Corn flakes	455	108
Crunchy nut corn flakes	500	119
Coco pops	465	111
Froot loops	490	116
Frosties	460	110
Honey smacks	485	115
Komplete natural	465	111
Oven baked	580	138
Just right	455	108
Nutri-grain	480	114
Puffed wheat	485	115
Rice bubbles	460	110

	kJ	Cals
Ready wheats	460	110
Special K	480	114
Sultana bran	360	86
Sustain	440	105
Toasted muesli	545	130

PURINA

	kJ	Cals
Bran, Nass processed	340	81
Natural	270	64
Processed	330	78
Fruit and bran flakes	390	93
Lite and natural	505	120
Muesli porridge	385	92
Swiss formula	415	98
Toasted muesli	560	134
Flakes	430	102
Hi-fibre	545	130

SANITARIUM

	kJ	Cals
Betta 'B' wheat germ	410	98
Bran bix	330	79
Bran cereal	315	75
Corn flakes	440	104
Crunchy granola	540	129
Fruit bran	340	81
Good start	430	103
Granola	425	101
Granose	400	96
Honey weets/puffs	450	108
Light 'n' tasty	425	101
Lite-bix	400	95
Muesli	560	134
Toasted	745	177
Unsweetened	575	137
Puffed wheat	430	103
Ricies	435	104
San bran	315	75
Wheat flakes	400	96

	kJ	Cals
Weet-bix	420	100
Hi-bran	410	97
Plus oat bran	410	97

WEIGHT WATCHERS

	kJ	Cals
Fruit and fibre	450	107
Muesli	450	107

CAKES

(average per slice)

	kJ	Cals
Banana cake, 100 g	1330	318
Black forest, 100 g	1440	343
Carrot cake, 100 g	1550	370
Cheesecake, average, 100 g	1740	415
Chocolate cake, home made, 100 g	1550	370
Fruitcake, dark, 100 g	1390	330
Light, 100 g	1430	340
Home prepared, average, 100 g	1350	325
Sponge, vanilla, commercial, 50 g	675	160
Vanilla, home made, 50 g	805	193
With jam and cream, 100 g	1300	310
Swiss roll, 50 g	685	164
Tea cake, 50 g	740	180

SMALL CAKES, BUNS, SLICES, TARTS (average, per cake)

	kJ	Cals
Baklava, 100 g	1540	368
Buns, cinnamon, 70 g	790	189
Fruit, glazed, 70 g	800	191
Iced, 70 g	870	208
Hot cross, 50 g	630	150

	kJ	Cals
Chocolate éclair, 60 g	940	225
Coconut slice, 100 g	1400	335
Cupcake, iced, 40 g	620	148
Custard tart, 100 g	1090	260
Danish pastry, 100 g	1290	310
Doughnut, cinnamon		
and sugar, 40 g	620	148
Iced, 40 g	710	170
Jam filled, 50 g	735	176
Fruit mince slice, iced,		
100 g	1250	300
Galactobureko, 100 g	880	210
Jam tart, 35 g,		
individual	565	135
¼ large, baked	1490	355
Lamington, 50 g	655	155
Meringue, 15 g	245	60
Vanilla slice, 100 g	855	205

Brand Names

SARA LEE (per 100 g)	kJ	Cals
Cakes, banana	1335	319
Carrot	1510	361
Chocolate	1450	346
Snack chocolate	1365	326
Gateaux, black forest	1340	321
Black forest double		
cream	1600	383
Carrot	1600	383
Celebration	1410	337
Chocolate on		
chocolate	1575	376
Double chocolate	1415	339
Hazelnut	1485	355
Mocca	1350	323
Strawberry	1315	315

	kJ	Cals
Swiss	1385	331
Walnut fudge	1285	308
Pound cakes, all		
purpose	1590	380
Apple pecan	1430	341
Chocolate	1550	371
Chocolate swirl	1484	355
Coconut	1430	342
Honey almond	1460	349
Snack	1460	350
Sultana	1550	371
Sponge cakes		
Chocolate	1220	292
Strawberry	1175	281
Passionfruit	1140	273

WHITE WINGS (prepared)	kJ	Cals
Country style,		
⅛ whole, 80 g		
serve		
Buttercake with		
vanilla frosting	1175	281
Carrot with cream		
cheese frosting	1235	295
Chocolate with		
chocolate frosting	1255	300
Chocolate chip with		
milk choc. frosting	1235	295
Family recipe,		
1/12 whole, 50 g		
serve		
Banana	590	141
Buttercake, chocolate	645	154
Golden	650	155
Sultana	750	180
Buttercup yellow	640	153
Date loaf	580	138
Gingerbread	630	151

	kJ	Cals
Madeira	690	165
Moist lemon	640	153
Orange	640	153
Rich chocolate	670	160
Swiss milk chocolate	640	153
Microwave moist, 50 g serve		
Chocolate	785	185
Choc-chip	930	220
Buttercake, sultana	875	210
Self icing, 50 g serve		
Banana with passionfruit icing	760	181
Carrot with honey icing	780	186
Chocolate with chocolate icing	800	191
Premium, black forest, 90 g	1085	259
Chocolate on chocolate, 80 g	1170	279
Lamingtons, 45 g	620	147
Lemon meringue pie, 100 g	1010	241
Triple chocolate, 90 g	1385	331
Sponge, 50 g serve		
Chocolate	710	169
Golden	680	162
Tea time treats		
Apple spice tea cake, 50 g	660	158
French tea cake, 50 g	660	158
Sixteens, 2 cakes, 25 g	480	115
Wholesome, 50 g serve		
Carrot	670	160
Coconut and banana	610	145
Orange and walnut	670	160

Pancakes

	kJ	Cals
Crepes, 15 cm diam., 20 g	250	60
Pancakes, 10 cm diam., 40 g	495	118
Pikelet, 6 cm diam., 15 g	190	45
Waffles, each, 30 g	175	40
Add: For 1 tsp butter	150	36
For 1 tsp jam	65	15
For 1 tsp whipped cream	110	26
For 1 tsp sugar	65	15
For 1 scoop ice cream	415	100

PANJACKS

	kJ	Cals
Plain, 2 pancakes, 60 g	630	150
With maple syrup	1410	336
Fruit pie, 1/6 average, baked	1030	245

Scones

	kJ	Cals
Scone, plain, home made, each, 50 g	725	173
Commercial, each, 50 g	565	135
Scone, fruit, home made, each, 50 g	725	173
Add: For 1 tsp butter	150	36
For 1 tsp jam	65	15
For 1 tsp whipped cream	110	26

FLOURS

	kJ	Cals
Arrowroot, 2 tbsp, 30 g	435	104
Carob, 2 tbsp, 30 g	480	115
Cornflour, 2½ tbsp, 30 g	470	112
Gravy powder, 2 tbsp, 30 g	600	145
Manioc, 3 tbsp, 30 g	400	95
Potato flour, 2½ tbsp, 30 g	450	107
Rice flour, 2 tbsp, 30 g	455	110
Rye, wholemeal, 1½ tbsp, 30 g	370	88
Soya flour, full fat, 2 tbsp, 30 g	560	134
Low fat, 2 tbsp, 30 g	445	107
Wheat, plain, 2 heaped tbsp, 30 g	440	105
Self raising, 2 heaped tbsp, 30 g	425	100
Wholemeal, 2 tbsp, 30 g	350	84

GRAINS

	kJ	Cals
Barley, pearl, boiled, ½ cup, 100 g	445	106
Raw, dry, 2 tbsp, 30 g	380	91
Buckwheat, dry, 2 tbsp, 30 g	435	104
Burgul (cracked wheat), boiled, ½ cup, 90 g	360	86
Raw, dry, 2 tbsp, 30 g	375	89
Soaked, 100 g	635	150
Maize/Millet meal, 3 tbsp, 30 g	460	110

	kJ	Cals
Matzo meal, 3 tbsp, 30 g	410	98
Polenta, dry, 30 g	415	100
Sago/Tapioca, dry, 2 tbsp, 30 g	455	110
Cooked in water, 100 g	120	30
Semolina, dry, 30 g	405	97

NOODLES

	kJ	Cals
Plain/Egg, boiled, 1 cup, 150 g	820	195
Dry, uncooked, 50 g	735	175
Instant, ½ sachet with flavouring	820	195
Stir fried, 1 cup, 150 g	1130	268
2 MINUTE NOODLES, 1 packet		
Beef	1655	395
Chicken	1625	388
Curry	1650	395
Fried Onion	1635	391
Oriental	1655	395
Prawn	1630	390

PASTA

	kJ	Cals
Cannelloni, average, dry, 1 tube, 10 g	140	33
Prepared with filling, 100 g	605	145
Lasagna, average, dry, 1 sheet, 20 g	280	65
Prepared with sauce, 100 g	545	130

	kJ	Cals
Soyaroni, boiled, 1 cup, 150 g	680	163
Dry, uncooked, 50 g	630	150
Spaghetti, Macaroni etc., white,		
Boiled, 1 cup, 150 g	740	175
Dry, uncooked, 50 g	715	170
Fresh, uncooked, 50 g	585	140
Wholemeal, boiled, 1 cup, 130 g	710	170
Dry, uncooked, 50 g	665	158
Spinach/Tomato flavoured		
Boiled, 1 cup, 150 g	810	193
Dry, uncooked, 50 g	745	177
Vegaroni, boiled, 1 cup, 120 g	530	127
Dry, uncooked, 50 g	660	158

PASTRY

(per 100 g, 1 sheet)

	kJ	Cals
Choux, raw	910	218
Baked	1400	335
Fillo, raw	1190	285
Baked	1560	373
Flaky, raw	1810	433
Baked	2380	570
Pizza base, each	3600	860
Puff, raw	1520	364
Baked	1870	447
Short, raw	1730	414
Baked	2050	490
Vol au vent, large, 10 cm, unfilled	300	72
Small, 4 cm, unfilled	35	8

	kJ	Cals
Wholemeal, raw	1350	323
Baked	1850	443

RICE

	kJ	Cals
White/quick cooking brown,		
Boiled/steamed, 1 cup, 150 g	780	185
Raw, dry, 30 g	440	105
Brown/wholemeal, Boiled/steamed,		
1 cup, 150 g	945	225
Raw, dry, 30 g	460	110
Fried, average, 1 cup, 130 g	1210	290
RICES OF THE WORLD,		
100 g, Chinese	600	143
Creole	605	144
Hawaiian	620	148
Indian	610	145
RICE PLUS, ½ cup serve		
Fried rice	725	173
Nasi Goreng	740	177
Pilaf	890	213
Risotto	540	129
Satay	930	222

CONDIMENTS, DIPS, SAUCES AND SPREADS

CONDIMENTS

PICKLES, RELISHES, MUSTARDS

(per tbsp, 20 g)	kJ	Cals
Branston pickles	135	32
Chutney, fruit	220	53
Low joule	60	14
Corn relish	85	20
Gherkin spread	125	30
Horseradish	60	14
Cream	135	32
Mustards,		
MASTERFOODS		
American	100	23
Australian	90	21
English, hot	130	31
Mild	85	20
French	90	21
German	80	19
Pickles, mustard,		
average	75	18
Sandwich relish		
(**KRAFT**)	130	31
Tomato relish	85	20

DIPS

CRACKA-DIP (BROWNES)

(per tbsp, 20 g)		
Bacon and onion	155	37
French onion	155	37
Malaysian satay	180	43
Spicy Mexican	155	37
Tangy gherkin	160	38

DAIRY FARMERS

	kJ	Cals
Bacon and tomato	185	44
French onion	175	42
Onion and bacon	175	42
Mexican taco	165	40
Seafood	167	40

LAWRY'S

Avocado	220	53
Bacon and onion	235	56
Cheese and bacon	305	73
Chive	225	54
Cucumber	250	60
French onion	245	59
Herb	240	58
Onion and garlic	235	56
Seafood	240	58

SOFT PHILADELPHIA (KRAFT)

Barbeque	205	49
French onion	210	50
Gherkin	215	51
Herb and garlic	240	57
Mild pepper	245	58
Onion and bacon	215	51
Smoked oyster	205	49
Spicy Mexican	210	50

SAUCES

Average, all brands (per tbsp, 20 g)	kJ	Cals
Apple sauce	35	8
Barbeque sauce	150	36
Cheese sauce	165	39
Chilli sauce	50	12
Gravy	105	25
Horseradish cream	175	42
HP sauce	80	19
Mint jelly	85	20
Mint sauce	60	14
Thick	80	18
Old English sauce	125	30
Pesto sauce	140	34
Plum sauce	155	37
Satay sauce	245	60
Soy sauce	30	8
Spicy plum sauce	115	28
Spicy red sauce	110	26
Steak sauce	125	30
Sugo, tomato pasta sauce	40	10
Sweet and sour sauce	170	40
Taco sauce	25	6
Tartare sauce	110	26
Teryaki sauce	80	20
Tomato paste	70	16
No added salt	70	16
Puree, 100 g	195	46
Sauce	85	20
Low joule	30	7
No added salt	85	20
White sauce, home made	115	28
Worcestershire sauce	60	15

Brand Names

FOUNTAIN (per tbsp, 20 g)	kJ	Cals
BBQ	120	28
Black bean	115	27
Chilli, hot	120	28
Mild	30	7
Mint	65	15
Mustard	110	26
Satay	160	38
Soy	110	26
Soy sauce with garlic	110	26
Spicy red	130	30
Steak	145	34
Sweet and sour	325	78
Teriyaki marinade and baste	150	36

GRAVOX (made up, per ¼ cup serve)	kJ	Cals
Gravox		
Chicken	50	12
Gravymaker	45	11
Light brown	50	12
Low joule, 50 ml	35	8
Supreme	45	11
Carvery gravy mix		
Beef with bouquet garni	90	21
Beef with mushroom	90	21
Chicken with bay and peppercorn	85	20
Chicken with sage and onion	85	20
Lamb with rosemary	85	20
Pork with caraway	90	21

CONDIMENTS, DIPS, SAUCES AND SPREADS

Gravyboat	kJ	Cals
Brown onion	90	21
Roast meat	90	21
Seasoned chicken	90	21
Traditional	95	22
Saucery sauce mix		
Brown onion	85	20
Cheese	200	47
Diane	165	40
Mushroom and garlic	170	41
Parsley	180	43
Pepper	180	43
White	175	42

KAN TONG		
(per tbsp, 20 g)		
Cajun	30	7
Mongolian sauce	70	17
Satay sauce	60	14
Teriyaki sauce	60	14

MASTERFOODS		
(per tbsp, 20 g)		
Chilli	45	11
Satay	210	50
Seafood cocktail	170	40
Soy	20	4
Sweet and sour	125	30
Tartare	485	115

McCORMICK		
Foil sauces		
(per pack)		
Beef marinade, 30 g	390	93
Chicken cacciatore, 40 g	515	123
Steak Dianne, 40 g	670	160
Tuna casserole, 40 g	445	106

Pasta Sauces

DOLMIO (per 100 g)	kJ	Cals
Chunky bolognaise		
Farmhouse vegetable	240	57
Garden vegetable	195	46
Onion and mushroom	205	48
Tomato, onion and garlic	180	43
Rich and hearty bolognaise		
Tomato	420	100
Tomato and eggplant	360	86
Tomato and olive	370	88
Traditional bolognaise		
Spicy peppers	215	51
Tomato	165	39
Tomato and capsicum	195	47
Tomato and cheese	255	60
Tomato and mushroom	200	48
Provinciale		
Fettucine alfredo	435	104
Macaroni napolitana	200	48
Spaghetti carbonara	505	121

EDGELL (per 100 g)		
Pasta sauce, plain	230	55
Bolognaise	310	74
Chunky vegetable	250	59
Marinara	300	72
Mushroom and		
tomato	245	58
Tomato and bacon	400	95
Spaghetti sauce	295	70

LEGGO (per 100 g)		
Italian Cooking Sauces		
Bolognaise with garlic		
and onions	245	58
With mild chilli	280	67

	kJ	Cals
Napolitana with mushrooms and herbs	265	63
Primavera chunky vegetable	260	62
Salsa di pomodoro	275	65
Traditional with basil and oregano	265	63
Tastes of Italy — Recipe Base		
Bolognaise with garlic and herbs	270	64
With wine and chilli	275	65
Cacciatora with herbs and onions	320	76
Parmigiana with cheese and herbs	280	66

PAUL NEWMAN (per 100 g)

	kJ	Cals
Marinara spaghetti sauce	235	56
Mushroom spaghetti sauce	235	56
Sockarooni spaghetti sauce	185	44

RAGULETTO (per 125 g serve)

	kJ	Cals
Basilico	150	36
Calabrese	155	37
Capri-style	235	56
Napolitana	270	64
Romano	260	62
Sicilian	245	58
Venetian	290	70

WEIGHT WATCHERS

	kJ	Cals
Pasta sauce, 100 g	200	47

Stir Fry Sauces

CORNWELLS EASTERN FEAST (per 100 g)

	kJ	Cals
Black bean sauce with vegetables	240	57
Plum sauce with vegetables	470	112
Satay sauce with vegetables	820	196
Sweet and sour sauce with vegetables	395	95

KAN TONG (per 100 g)

	kJ	Cals
Black bean sauce with vegetables	215	51
Lemon honey sauce with vegetables	290	69
Mild curry sauce with vegetables	230	55
Peanut curry sauce with vegetables	330	79
Red curry sauce with vegetables	255	61
Spicy plum sauce with vegetables	335	80
Sweet and sour sauce with vegetables	420	100

SPREADS

Savoury

	kJ	Cals
Butter/margarine, 1 tsp, 5 g	150	36
Fish spread, average, 1 tbsp, 20 g	160	38

	kJ	Cals
Salmon and shrimp/ salmon and anchovy/ salmon, herring and tomato	120	29
Salmon, crab and tomato	105	25
Liverwurst, 1 tbsp, 25 g	275	66
Marmite, ½ tsp, 3 g	20	5
Meat paste, average, 1 tbsp, 20 g	170	41
Natex yeast extract (Nestle), 1 tsp, 5 g	45	11
Pâté, average, 1tbsp, 25 g	250	60
Peanut butter, average, 1 tbsp, 20 g	490	117
Unsweetened, 1 tbsp	500	120
Sandwich relish, (**KRAFT**), 2 tsp, 10 g	60	15
Sandwich spreads:		
KRAFT, 2 tsp, 10 g		
Beef, ham and chicken	80	19
Beef, veal and bacon	80	19
Devilled beef and ham	85	21
MASTERFOODS, 2 tsp, 10 g		
Chicken and beef	90	22
Corn 'n' bacon	45	10
Devilled chicken	80	19
Ham	70	17
Salmon	75	18
Peppered steak	85	20

	kJ	Cals
Tahini, 1 tbsp, 25 g	655	156
Vegemite, ½ tsp, 5 g	20	5

Sweet

(per tbsp, 20 g)	kJ	Cals
Chocolate spread e.g. Ferrero	500	120
Fruit mince	230	55
With rum	235	56
Fruit spreads, sugarless e.g. country harvest	150	36
Jam, average	300	72
Low-joule, average	20	5
COTTEES		
Boysenberry	20	5
Breakfast	10	3
Raspberry	20	5
Strawberry	15	4
WEIGHT WATCHERS		
Apricot	25	6
Marmalade	15	4
Plum	25	6
Raspberry	30	7
Strawberry	20	5
Golden syrup	380	90
Honey	300	72
Lemon/orange spread/ butter	250	60
Marmalade, average	335	80
Low joule, average	20	5

CONFECTIONERY

CHOCOLATE BARS

CADBURY	kJ	Cals
Caramel koala, 20 g	415	99
Cherry ripe 55 g	1010	242
Chomp 30 g		
Caramel	600	143
Choc orange	600	143
Peppermint	600	143
Crunchie, 50 g	1005	240
Curly wurly bar, 25 g	515	123
Dairy milk, 15 g	330	78
Farm friends, white,		
15 g	350	84
Flake, 30 g	665	158
Fruit and nut slab, 55 g	1120	268
Frys, cream, 45 g	810	194
Five fruits, 45 g	810	194
Turkish delight, 55 g	885	211
Furry friends, 15 g	330	78
Freddo, fudgee, 20 g	430	103
Milk, 15 g	330	78
Milky white, 15 g	350	84
Peppermint, 20 g	405	97
Rainbow chip, 15 g	320	77
Garfield, caramel, 20 g	410	98
Honeycomb, 15 g	320	77
Milk, 20 g	440	105
Moro, 65 g	1210	289
Almond, 55 g	1110	265
Peanut, 55 g	1105	264
Peanut slab, 55 g	1260	300
Picnic, 50 g	1060	254
Twirl, 35 g	785	187
Whip, 70 g	1335	319

MARS	kJ	Cals
Bounty, single, 60 g	1200	287
Fun sized, 28 g	560	134
Mars bar, single, 60 g	1108	265
Fun sized, 21 g	510	124
Milky way, single, 30 g	540	129
Fun sized, 16 g	290	69
M & M's plain, 50 g	1000	239
Peanut, 50 g	1050	251
Snickers, single, 60 g	1175	281
Fun sized, 16 g	315	75

MASTERCRAFT		
Bobbies	430	102
Golden rough	545	130
Kurls	430	102
Mint patties	425	102
Scorched peanut bar	800	191

NESTLÉ		
Chokito bar	1035	248
Milo bar	405	98

ROWNTREE		
Aero, milk, 30 g	650	156
Peppermint, 30 g	675	162
White, 30 g	675	162
Bertie beetle, 10 g		
Coffee crisp, 45 g	940	225
Drifter, 50 g	980	235
Kit kat, 45 g	940	225
Peppermint crisp, 35 g	685	163
Pollywaffle, 50 g	978	234
Tosca, 45 g	760	182
Violet crumble, 50 g	950	228
White knights, 25 g	435	104

CHOCOLATE BLOCKS

	kJ	Cals
Average, 1 square, 6 g	130	32
5 pieces, 30 g	660	158
1 55 g block	1210	290
1 100 g block	2200	525
1 250 g block	5500	1315
1 375 g block	8250	1973
Filled block, average,		
1 large square,		
10 g	200	48
3 large squares, 30 g	600	144

CADBURY
(per 30 g, average 5 squares)

Brazil nut	670	160
Caramello	590	140
Cashews	670	160
Chocolate truffle	630	150
Coconut delight	665	159
Crisp	725	174
Dairy milk	660	157
Energy	640	152
English toffee truffle	595	141
Fruit and nut	610	145
Hazel nut	625	149
Macadamia nut	665	159
Nut mix	655	156
Old Jamaica	575	137
Peppermint, dark	570	136
Milk	590	140
Premium dark	630	150
Roast almond	665	159
Snack	590	140
Swiss chalet	640	153
Top deck	680	162
White	705	168
White Swiss chalet	670	160

CHOCOLATES — VARIOUS

	kJ	Cals
After dinner mint,		
1 average, 5 g	125	30
Boxes, average,		
1 chocolate, 8 g	140	33
Black magic, 125 g box	2050	490
Dairy box, 125 g box	2310	553
Elegance, dark,		
250 g box	4265	1020
Milk, 250 g box	4390	1050
Quality Street, 185 g		
carton	3095	740
Chocolate coated,		
Almonds, 30 g	650	155
Peanuts, 30 g	650	155
Sultanas, 30 g	500	120
Liqueur cherry, 10 g	200	48
Rocky road, 30 g	585	140
DARRELL LEA		
Bo peep, 50 g	630	150
Chocolate almond		
nougat bar, 45 g	550	132
Chocolate caramel		
snows, 100 g	1420	340
Chocolate ginger, 100 g	1040	248
Chocolate log, 45 g	765	183
Chocolate peppermint		
bar, 40 g	460	110
Chocolate walnut roll,		
170 g	2200	526
Liquorice, 100 g	1115	266
Peanut brittle, 100 g	1730	413
Rocklea road, 100 g	1625	388
Toasted marshmallow,		
100 g	1555	372

LOLLIES/SWEETS

**ALLENS/CADBURY/LIFESAVER/
PASCALL/ROWNTREE/SCANLENS/
MASTERCRAFT
(per lolly)**

	kJ	Cals
Alphabet candy	65	16
Animal jellies	70	17
Aniseed and honey	65	16
Aniseed rings	65	16
Chocolate coated	100	24
Anticol	65	16
Ball gum	120	29
Bananas	65	16
Banana split bar	335	80
Barley sugar	70	17
Bats	450	108
Black cats	55	13
Black crows	35	9
Boas	450	108
Bobbies	430	102
Boomerangs	65	16
Bottles galore	65	16
Bubble yum	105	25
Butter menthols,		
round	40	10
Square	65	16
Butter mints	65	16
Butterscotch, round	45	11
Callard and Bowsers		
chews	65	16
Caramel buds	40	10
Cheeky chats	37	9
Chicos, large	55	13
Choc buds	35	8
Chocky bears	55	13
Chocky creams	65	16

	kJ	Cals
Chocolate bullets	50	12
Chocolate chews	65	16
Chocolate éclairs	90	22
Choo choo bar	335	80
Chupa chups	125	30
Clicketies	25	6
Clinkers	80	19
Coconut quivers	90	22
Columbines	70	17
Country mints	95	23
Creamy caramels	80	19
Dongers	230	55
E.S. mints	45	11
Eucol	65	16
Fantales	85	20
Fieldberries	30	7
Freckles	40	10
Freshie lemon rollers	35	8
Frisco jubes	40	10
Fruit bon bons	85	20
Fruit drops	80	19
Fruit gums/pastilles	30	7
Fruit jellies	30	7
Fruit tingles	35	8
Glucojels	55	13
Golden rough	545	130
Hawaiian crunch,		
per 10 g	170	40
Honey bears	30	7
Honey and		
eucalyptus	65	16
Honeycomb, 10 g	170	40
Hubba bubba	105	25
Humphrey B. Bear	65	16
Irish moss	30	7
Jaffas	60	15
Jellies	65	16

	kJ	Cals		kJ	Cals
Jelly babies	60	15	Orange and lemon		
Jelly beans, large	55	13	slices	55	13
Small	30	7	Orange sherbies	85	20
Joggers	55	13	Ovalteenies	23	5
Jubes	70	17	Pineapples	55	13
Killer pythons	595	143	Pink panther bar	335	80
Killer toads	145	35	Pinkies	340	81
King frogs	250	60	Pythons	410	98
Knock knocks	82	20	Quick ease	25	6
Kool caramels	55	13	Racing cars	65	16
Kool chocs	60	15	Raspberries	30	7
Kool fruits	60	15	Raspberry fizz	65	16
Kool mints	60	15	Redskins bar	335	80
Kurls	430	103	Scorched peanut bar	800	191
Licorice, per 10 g	125	30	Smarties, single	20	6
Licorice allsorts	110	26	25 g pack	540	130
Licorice blocks	70	17	Snakes alive	95	23
Licorice chews	65	16	Snowball	525	125
Licorice twist	300	72	Soothers	65	16
Licorice yards	675	162	Spearmint leaves small	20	6
Lifesavers, average	30	7	Large	85	20
Malted milks	80	19	Starfish	50	12
Marshmallows	80	19	Steam rollers	40	10
Merry mints	110	26	Strawberries and cream	55	13
Metro gum, small	45	11	Strawberry malts	80	20
Super Metro	105	25	Sweet 'n' sour	65	16
Milk bottles	55	13	Tarzan jubes	30	7
Flavoured	65	16	Tennis racquets	55	13
Milky buds	35	8	Throaties	25	6
Milky frogs	250	60	Tic tacs	5	1
Minties	70	17	Tingly fruits	35	8
Mint patties	425	102	Toffee apple bar	335	80
Monster mouse	595	143	Toffee chocs	80	20
Musk rollers	40	10	Tropical fish	70	17
Musk stick	180	43	White knight	480	115
Nougat fruits	60	15	Wildberries	30	7
Occa roos	140	34	XXXX Mints	80	20

DAIRY PRODUCTS

CHEESE

CHEDDAR	kJ	Cals
Cheddar, average (Bega, Bodalla, Colby, Coon, Crackerbarrel, Mil-Lel, Robertson)		
3 cm cube, 30 g	500	120
½ cup, grated, 60 g	1000	240
Small block, 250 g	4165	995
Large block, 500 g	8330	1995
Cheddar, fat reduced (various brands)		
3 cm cube, 30 g	410	97
Salt reduced, 3 cm cube, 30 g	515	123
Fat & salt reduced, 3 cm cube, 30 g	430	103

PROCESSED CHEESES, (KRAFT, MOO)

	kJ	Cals
3 cm cube, 30 g	400	95
Kraft singles (24% fat), 21 g	265	63
Kraft 'Light' (16% fat), 21 g	215	50
Moo square	220	53
Flavoured processed, average, 30 g	400	95

OTHER CHEESES
(3 cm cube, 30 g)

	kJ	Cals
Babybel, bonbel	375	95
Blue castello	450	108

	kJ	Cals
Blue vein	465	111
Brie	420	100
Camembert	380	90
Cheedam	440	105
Cheese spread, see **Cheese Spreads**		
Cheshire	485	115
Colby	485	115
Cottage cheese, see **Lower Fat Cheeses**		
Cotto	265	63
Cream cheese, see **Cream Cheeses**		
Edam, average	445	106
Fat reduced	385	92

	kJ	Cals
Emmenthal	450	108
Farm	425	100
Feta, average	350	83
Low salt	470	112
Reduced fat (Jalna)	290	70
Fruit cheese, average	370	88
Fynbo	450	108
Gloucester	510	120
Gorgonzola	450	108
Gouda, average	480	114
Fat reduced	420	100
Haloumy	305	73
Havarti	510	122
Jalna, Polish	150	36
Slicing	150	36
Slimming	130	30
Jarlsburg	380	90
Mozzarella, average	380	90
Reduced fat	360	86
Muenster	450	108
Neufchatel, see **Cream Cheeses**		
Nimbin	500	119
Parmesan, 2 tbsp grated	555	132
Pecorino	445	105
Pepato	475	115
Pizza cheese	390	93
Provolone	455	109
Quark, see **Lower Fat Cheeses**		
Raclette	460	110
Ricotta, see **Lower Fat Cheeses**		
Romano	470	112
Samsoe	490	115
St Claire	460	110

	kJ	Cals
Steppen	405	96
Stilton	575	138
Swiss, average	475	115
Fat reduced	430	103
Tilsit	465	111

Cream Cheeses

	kJ	Cals
Average, 30 g	425	102
Mascarpone, 30 g	500	120
Neufchatel, plain, 30 g	325	78
Chocolate, 30 g	480	115
Strawberry, 30 g	425	102
Philadelphia cream cheese and soft cream cheese (33% fat) 30 g	430	103
½ cup, 125 g	1790	430
1 cup, 250 g	3580	855
Philadelphia light cream cheese (16% fat) 30 g	245	59
Riviana fruit cheese, 30 g		
Nuts and cognac	415	99
Pepper and cognac	415	99
Poppy seed	405	97
Riviana roll, 30 g		
Brandied orange	470	112
Pepper	425	101
Rum	470	112
Riviana Swirle, 30 g		
Bacon and onion	475	113
Chive	460	110
Dutch smoked, processed	425	101
Herb and garlic	465	111
Pepper	455	109

DAIRY PRODUCTS

Lower Fat Cheeses

COTTAGE CHEESE (average, all types)	kJ	Cals
2 tbsp, 30 g	185	45
½ cup, 100 g	620	148
Low fat, 2 tbsp, 30 g	115	28
½ cup, 100 g	385	92
Creamed cottage cheese, average all types		
2 tbsp, 30 g	155	37
½ cup, 100 g	510	122
Low fat, 2 tbsp, 30 g	125	30
½ cup, 100 g	420	100

BROWNES (per ½ cup, 100 g)		
Cottage cheese, skim milk	340	80
Low fat cottage cheese, celery, onion & gherkin	380	90
Curry	395	95
Tropical fruit	350	84
Chilli	365	87
Garden salad	355	85
Creamed cottage cheese, plain	440	105
Chives	440	104
Gherkin	440	105
Pineapple	500	120

RICOTTA CHEESE (average all types)		
2 tbsp, 30 g	185	44
Reduced fat, 2 tbsp, 30 g	160	38

QUARK	kJ	Cals
Jalna low-fat, 1½ tbsp, 30 g	135	32
Non-fat, 1½ tbsp, 30 g	80	19

No Fat Cheeses

	kJ	Cals
Lite chol (United Dairies), 30 g	345	83
Lo chol, 30 g	450	108

Spreads

KRAFT (per tbsp, 20 g)		
Cheddar cheese spread	260	62
Cheese spread & onion	245	58
Cream cheese spread	305	73

CREAM

	kJ	Cals
Pure, 48% fat, 1 tbsp, 20 ml	280	67
300 ml container	4200	1005
Reduced, 25% fat, 1 tbsp, 20 ml	220	53
300 ml container	3300	790
Sour, 35% fat, 1 tbsp, 20 ml	295	70
300 ml container	4425	1060
Sour, reduced, 18% fat, 1 tbsp, 20 ml	180	43
300 ml container	2700	645
Thickened, 35% fat, 1 tbsp, 20 ml	290	70
300 ml container	4320	1033
Whipped, average, 1 heaped tbsp	290	70

DAIRY PRODUCTS

Brand Names

BULLA	kJ	Cals
Sour light cream, 30 ml	250	60

DAIRY FARMERS
(per 30 ml)

	kJ	Cals
Cream	420	100
Cream, thickened	420	100
Cream, thickened, UHT	426	101
Sour cream	420	100
Sour light cream	250	60

FARMERS UNION

	kJ	Cals
Light sour, 30 ml	250	60
Rich, 30 ml	585	140
Scalded, 30 ml	585	140
Thickened, 30 ml	440	105

MEADOW GOLD

	kJ	Cals
Cream, pure, 30 ml	530	126
thickened, 30 ml	410	98
Sour light cream, 30 ml	290	70

NO FRILLS

	kJ	Cals
Thickened cream, 30 ml	435	104

NORCO

	kJ	Cals
Sour cream, 30 ml	445	106
Thickened cream, 30 ml	435	104

OAK

	kJ	Cals
Sour light cream, 1 tbsp, 20 ml	165	40
Thickened, 1 tbsp, 20 ml	290	70
300 ml container	4350	1040

WEIGHT WATCHERS

	kJ	Cals
Extra lite sour cream, 1 tbsp, 20 ml	140	34

MILK

MILK — FRESH OR UHT	kJ	Cals
Whole, 1 tbsp, 20 ml	55	15
1 glass, 200 ml	540	130
300 ml carton	815	195
600 ml carton	1630	390
1 litre	2710	650
Reduced fat, protein increased,		
1 tbsp, 20 ml	45	10
1 glass, 200 ml	450	110
600 ml carton	1350	325
1 litre	2250	540
Skim, 1 tbsp, 20 ml	40	10
1 glass, 200 ml	325	80
l litre	1630	390

Flavoured Milks

	kJ	Cals
Average, 300 ml	1080	260
600 ml carton	2160	520
Milkshake, average, 200 ml	1020	245
Smoothie, average, 200 ml	950	230
Thickshake, average, 200 ml	910	215

EVAPORATED, CONDENSED
AND POWDERED MILK

	kJ	Cals
Condensed: Sweetened, 1 tbsp 20 ml	275	65
Skim, sweetened, 1 tbsp, 20 ml	225	55
Condensed: Coffee & milk, 1 tbsp	335	80
Evaporated: 1 tbsp, 20 ml	120	30
Reduced fat, 1 tbsp, 20 ml	80	20

	kJ	Cals
Skim, 1 tbsp, 20 ml	65	15
Powdered: Full cream, 2 tbsp, 15 g	310	75
Skim, 2 tbsp, 15 g	220	55

OTHER MILK

	kJ	Cals
Buttermilk, 1 glass, 200 ml	380	90
Coconut milk/water, 1 glass, 200 ml	170	40
Goat milk, 1 glass, 200 ml	415	100
Human milk, 200 ml	580	138

SOY BEAN MILK

	kJ	Cals
Average, 1 glass, 200 ml	560	135
So Good, Tetra-Pak, 250 ml	650	155
Caramel	750	179
Honeycomb	750	179
Jaffa	750	179
Strawberry	750	179
Lite, 1 glass, 200 ml	360	86
Soypreme, 200 ml	600	143
Vanilla	600	143

Brand Names

BEAR BRAND

	kJ	Cals
Evaporated milk, 1 tbsp, 20 ml	130	30
Reduced fat, 1 tbsp, 20 ml	80	20

CARNATION

	kJ	Cals
Coffee mate, 1 tsp.	45	10
Evaporated milk, 1 tbsp, 20 ml	130	30

	kJ	Cals
Evaporated skim milk, 1 tbsp, 20 ml	65	15
Sweetened condensed milk, 1 tbsp	350	85
Sweetened condensed skim milk, 1 tbsp	310	75
Skim milk powder, 10 g	150	35

DAIRY FARMERS

Flavoured Milk (per 300 ml)

	kJ	Cals
Good One		
Carob	1165	280
Honey & malt	1160	278
Muesli	1130	270
Moove		
Caramel	940	225
Chocolate	920	220
Coffee	900	215
Strawberry	995	235
Moove, UHT		
Chocolate	980	234
Coffee	950	227
Strawberry	995	236
Real		
Chocolate, fresh	965	230
UHT	820	196
Coffee, fresh	955	229
UHT	800	191
Strawberry, fresh	955	229
UHT	835	200

DIPLOMA

	kJ	Cals
Challenge, 100 ml made up	245	60

	kJ	Cals
FARMERS UNION		
Flavoured Milk		
(per 300 ml)		
Choc shake low fat	910	217
Classic chocolate	1165	278
Egg nog	1495	356
Iced coffee low fat	890	211
Strawberry shake low fat	855	204
UHT flavoured low fat	855	204
NESTLES		
Flavoured Milk		
Milo, 250 ml	880	210
Quik, chocolate, 250 ml	920	210
Strawberry, 250 ml	965	230
Vienna coffee, 250 ml	850	205
Powdered Milk		
Slender reduced fat milk powder 2 tbsp, 15 g	270	65
Sunshine full cream powder, 2 tbsp, 15 g	300	70
NIPPY'S		
Average all flavours, 375 ml	1050	250
NORCO		
Milk		
Lite white, reduced fat, 100 ml	220	52
Milk, whole, 100 ml	280	67
Flavoured Milk		
Average, 200 ml	660	158
Cereal delight, 200 ml	620	148

	kJ	Cals
PHYSICAL		
Ultra-filtered milk, 100 ml	210	50
SPRING VALLEY		
Flavoured Milk		
Baco liquid lunch, 250 ml		
Chocolate	1165	278
Vanilla malt	1155	275
Baco luxury, reduced fat, 375 ml		
Chocolate	1000	240
Coffee	930	222
Strawberry	945	226
UNITED DAIRIES		
(per 100 ml)		
Hi-Lo	240	57
Milk, whole	285	68
Skim	145	35
Shape	195	47
VICTORIAN DAIRY INDUSTRY AUTHORITY		
Milk		
(per 100 ml)		
Farmhouse, enriched	315	75
New skinny	165	40
Milk, whole	280	65
Rev	210	50
Revital	280	65
Flavoured milk		
(per 300 ml)		
Big M, fresh and UHT	980	235
Big M, egg flip	1240	295

YOGHURT

	kJ	Cals
(average per 200 g carton)		
Natural	650	154
Low fat	430	100
Fruit flavoured	840	200
Low fat	810	193

Brand Names

(per 200 g carton)	kJ	Cals
ATTIKI		
Country Style	630	150
Low fat fruit: apple, cherry, honey, strawberry	370	88
Natural	290	69
Sylvarian	705	168
BROWNES		
Natural	670	160
Strawberry	810	194
Apricot	740	177
Tropical fruit	735	176
Vanilla	910	217
With spicy apple	925	220
With cherry & coconut	1000	240
DAIRY FARMERS		
Traditional natural	645	154
With honey	815	195
Vanilla	880	210
Natural, low fat	425	100

	kJ	Cals
DANONE		
Diet lite	375	90
Fruit yoghurt, mixed berry	815	195
Other fruits	775	185
Lite & fruity, all flavours	605	145
Danino, fruit, average, per 150 g carton	560	135
PAULS		
Extra fruit, strawberry/ fruit salad	775	185
Mixed berry, vanilla & peach	815	195
Real fruit, average	810	194
Low fat, plain	440	106
fruit	605	144
SILHOUETTE		
Fruit of the forest	425	102
Fruit salad	435	104
Mango and kiwi fruit	410	98
Strawberry	420	100
SKI		
Fruit Yogurt		
Apricot	760	180
Forest fruit	835	200
Fruit salad	820	195
Orange & apricot	820	195
Passionfruit/strawberry	805	192
Raspberry	790	189
Light Yoghurt		
Apricot	625	149
Berries & cherries	710	170
Mango & peach	640	152
Strawberry	670	160
Tropical fruit	650	155

DAIRY PRODUCTS

79

	kJ	Cals		kJ	Cals
YOMIX			Blueberry	705	168
Natural	430	100	Fruit of the forest	720	172
Apricot/blueberry/			Fruit salad	720	172
raspberry	630	150	Peach and cherry	715	170
Banana/strawberry	650	155	Strawberry	680	165
Blackforest	660	157	Strawberry and banana	685	166
Fruit salad	670	160	Strawberry and guava	705	168
			Strawberry and peach	700	167
YOPLAIT			Tropical fruit	720	172
(per 200 g serve)					
Original			**YOPLUS**		
Apricot	760	182	Apricot	735	180
Banana	810	193	Blueberry	745	178
Banana and			Fruit tango	740	177
passionpeach	790	189	Natural 100%	690	164
Fruit of the forest	795	190	Strawberry	725	173
Fruit salad	795	190			
Fruit tango	770	184	**WEIGHT WATCHERS**		
Kiwi fruit and mango	785	188	Natural, skim milk	410	98
Orchard fruit	790	189	Fruit salad	395	95
Peach and guava	780	186	Grapefruit/mandarin	430	102
Pineapple and mandarin	740	177	Strawberry	385	92
Redberry cocktail	770	184			
Strawberry	760	182			
Strawberry and banana	780	186			
Tropical fruit	790	189			
Vanilla	955	228			
Vanilla and blackberry	810	193			
Vanilla and dark plum	820	196			
Vanilla and hazelnut	890	213			
Low Fat					
Apricot	690	165			
Apricot, pear and					
passionfruit	720	172			
banana, apple and					
cinnamon	720	172			
Banana and honey	690	165			
Banana and mandarin	680	163			

DAIRY PRODUCTS

DESSERTS AND PUDDINGS

CUSTARDS AND DAIRY DESSERTS

> Custard is made from milk, egg and sugar. A similar product is labelled a 'dairy dessert' because it does not contain sufficient egg to qualify it as 'custard'.

Average all brands	kJ	Cals
Custard powder, dry, 2 tbsp, 20 g	285	68
Custard, prepared with milk, ½ cup, 125 ml	510	122
Custard, ready made, average, ½ cup, 125 ml	525	125
Egg custard, prepared with milk, ¼ serve of 75 g pack	750	179
Quick custard, prepared with milk, ¼ serve of 80 g pack	335	80
Homemade baked, ½ cup, 125 g	550	130
With skim milk, ½ cup, 125 g	400	95
Homemade with custard powder, ½ cup, 125 g	510	122
With skim milk, ½ cup, 125 g	350	84

Brand Names

BINGO

	kJ	Cals
Custard powder, 2 tbsp, 20 g	280	67

	kJ	Cals
Egg custard, ¼ serve made from 75 g pack	750	179

DAIRY FARMERS

UHT dairy dessert, average all flavours, ½ cup, 125 ml	530	130
Vanilla custard, ½ cup, 125 ml	520	125

DAIRY VALE

Custard, ½ cup, 125 ml	375	90

FOSTER CLARKS

Custard powder, 2 tbsp, 20 g	280	67
Egg custard, ¼ serve made from 75 g pack	750	179
Quick custard, ¼ serve made from 80 g pack	335	80

NORDICA

Custard, all flavours, ½ cup, 125 ml	550	130

DESSERTS AND PUDDINGS

OAK	kJ	Cals
Custard, ½ cup, 125 ml	550	130
Dairy Dessert, ½ cup, 125 ml	735	175

PAULS

	kJ	Cals
Custard, ½ cup, 125 ml	580	140

PETERS FARM

Yogo, average, 200 g carton	890	215
Banana/caramel	895	215
Strawberry	895	215
Chocolate	870	208

SNAK PACK (per 150 g serve)

	kJ	Cals
Banana	790	189
Caramel	785	188
Chocolate	795	190
Double Chocolate	805	193
Strawberry	795	190
Vanilla	790	189

DESSERTS AND PUDDINGS

	kJ	Cals
Apple strudel, average, 125 g piece	1020	245
Chocolate mousse, average, ½ cup, 125 g	720	170
Fromage frais (fruche, frubelle), 200 g carton	930	220
Lemon meringue pie, ⅛ whole, 90 g	820	195

Pavlova, ⅛ medium, 125 g	kJ 950	Cals 230
Pavlova magic mix, prepared, ⅙ serve of 125 g	675	160
With cream and fruit	1000	240
Plum pudding, average, 100g piece	1150	275
Rice cream, average, ½ cup, 100 g	570	135
Trifle, average, ½ cup, 120 g	870	210

Brand Names

BROWNES (per 120 ml serve) Pure Indulgence

	kJ	Cals
Chocolate mousse	780	187
Coffee mousse	765	183
Lemon mousse	775	186
Strawberry mousse	775	186

COTTEES

Instant puddings, average, ½ cup	555	133

COUNTRY FAIR

Lemon meringue pie, ⅙ whole, 100 g	1010	240

FARMLAND

Chocolate Bavarian, ⅙ whole, 100 g	1360	324
Cheese cake, ⅙ whole, 100 g	1510	360
Strawberry cheese cake, ⅙ whole, 100 g	1230	293

82

NANNA'S (per 100 g)	kJ	Cals
Apple Roll	800	191
Pies		
Apple	850	203
Apricot	940	224
Blackberry/apple	1070	255
Cinnamon/apple	945	226
Rhubarb/apple	950	226
Snack		
Apple pie	995	237
Apple/custard pie	910	217
Apricot pie	1020	242
Blackberry/apple pie	1060	253
Blueberry/apple pie	1100	263
Spicy apple pie	995	237
Strudel		
Apple	890	213
Blueberry/apple	1010	241
Danish/apple	875	209
Sultana/cream	1365	325
Tropical dessert	1010	240
Waffles	575	137

FOUR 'N' TWENTY (per 100 g)	kJ	Cals
Apple pie	1000	238
Apricot pie	1090	261
Boysenberry pie	1030	246

PAMPAS (per 100 g)	kJ	Cals
Apple puffs	1085	259
Apple strudel	735	176
Apricot puffs	1065	254
Berry puffs	1130	270
Blackberry meringue	1000	238
Self serve	1035	247
Lemon meringue	1045	250
Self serve	1080	259

SARA LEE (per 100 g)	kJ	Cals
Cheesecakes		
Blueberry	1120	268
Cherry	1090	261
Original	1060	254
Strawberry	1090	261
Dairy Desserts		
Chocolate Bavarian	1460	349
Chocolate chip Bavarian	1330	318
French cream cheese	1330	318
Danish		
Apple	1100	263
Apple pullapart	1305	312
Apricot	1005	240
Blueberry	1060	254
Cherry	1040	249
Pecan	1580	378
Lights		
Chocolate mousse	810	194
French cream cheese, berry	770	184
Strawberry	770	184
Pies and Hi Pies		
Apple pie	1150	275
Apple hi pie	980	234
Apricot pie	1150	275
Blackberry hi pie	1090	261
Blueberry pie	1130	270
Cherry pie	1180	282

WHITE WINGS		
Bavarian Creme (¼ whole, 55 g serve)		
Choc-Mint	365	87
Mocha	355	85

Cheesecakes (80 g serve)	kJ	Cals
Continental	1105	264
Chocolate	1100	263
Lemon	1010	242
Fruit Salad	980	235
Instant Puddings (⅙ whole, 115 g serve)		
Chocolate	500	120
Strawberry	545	130
Vanilla	545	130
Microwave Moist Self Saucing Sponge Puddings (150 g serve)		
Blackberry	1755	419
Butterscotch	1765	422
Chocolate	1755	419
Lemon	1755	419
Real Fruit Dessert (per 125 g serve)		
Apricot	400	96
Mango	430	102
Strawberry	405	97
Tropical	410	98
Pie Filling Mix (prepared, per 100 g)		
Lemon	370	89
Self Saucing Sponge Puddings (¼ whole, 125 g serve)		
Apricot	1015	240
Blackberry	1015	240
Butterscotch	1015	240
Chocolate	1085	260
Lemon	1015	240
Other		
Chocolate mousse, per ¼ whole, 75 g	350	84

	kJ	Cals
Creme caramel, per ¼ whole, 185 g	880	210
Lemon meringue pie, 100 g serve	1010	241

DESSERT TOPPINGS

(per tbsp 20 ml)	kJ	Cals
Chocolate fudge/ caramel	600	145
Syrup toppings, average	200	50
COTTEES		
Banana/raspberry/ strawberry	170	40
Caramel/lime/vanilla	210	50
Chocolate/choc malt	230	55
Ice magic	580	140
Low-joule, caramel	20	5
Chocolate	17	4
Strawberry	10	3
WEIGHT WATCHERS		
Low-joule, fruity apricot	15	4
Fruity strawberry	15	4
Rich chocolate	25	6

JELLIES

	kJ	Cals
Gelatine, dry, 3 tsp, 10 g (1 sachet)	125	30
Jelly, average, prepared, ½ cup, 100 g	350	83
Low joule, average, ½ cup, 100 g	35	8
Junket, per tablet	10	2

Brand Names

AEROPLANE JELLY (½ cup, 100 g)	kJ	Cals
Jelly, prepared	315	75
Low joule, prepared	30	5

COTTEES		

Average all flavours,
     prepared, ½ cup,
     100 g
	315	75

Diet jelly crystals, per serve, 125 g		
Lemon	30	7
Lime	30	7
Orange	30	7
Raspberry	30	7
Strawberry	30	7

GOLD CREST		

Average all flavours,
     prepared, ½ cup,
     100 g
	280	70

Low joule, prepared, ½ cup, 100 g	35	10

PIONEER (per 125 g serve)		
Low joule jellies, per serve, 125 g		
Lemon	30	7
Lime	30	7
Orange	30	7
Pineapple	30	7
Raspberry	30	7
Strawberry	30	7

YOMIX		
Jelly cup, 150 g tub	565	135

EGGS

CHICKEN	kJ	Cals
Eggs, raw, boiled, poached		
Small, 49 g	290	70
Medium, 55 g	330	80
Large, 60 g	355	85
Jumbo, 65 g	385	90
Egg white, 55 g egg	110	25
Egg yolk, 55 g egg	220	50

OTHER

Duck, 70 g	540	130
Goose, 150 g	1125	270
Quail, 10 g	65	15
Turkey, 85 g	570	135

EGG SUBSTITUTES

Country harvest egg replacing powder 1 tbsp, 10 g	125	30
Scrambler's cholesterol free, frozen 1 sachet (2 eggs), 100 g	680	160

COOKED EGGS

Fried, average, 55 g egg	580	140
Omelette, 2 eggs, 20 g cheese, milk	1210	290
Scrambled, 2 × 55 g eggs, 2 tbsp milk	770	185

EGG AND CHEESE DISHES

Cauliflower cheese, 100 g	470	110
Cheese souffle, 100 g	1030	245
Macaroni cheese, 100 g	725	175
Quiche, 100 g	1625	390

FATS AND OILS

	kJ	Cals
Butter, all brands,		
5 g (1 tsp)	150	36
20 g (1 tbsp)	610	144
125 g (½ cup)	3800	905
Copha, 125 g (½ cup)	4625	1100
Cream, see **Dairy Products**		
Dripping, beef, 100 g	3700	880
Fat, solid, frying 100 g	3700	880
Garlic and herb butter/ margarine, 1 tsp	150	35
Margarine, regular,		
5 g (1 tsp)	150	35
20 g (1 tbsp)	600	143
125 g (½ cup)	3750	893
Margarine, light, average, 5 g (1 tsp)	80	19
Oil (canola, fish oil, grapeseed, maize, olive, peanut, safflower, sesame, soybean, sunflower, blended vegetable)		
1 tsp, 5 ml	185	45
1 tbsp, 20 ml	740	177
½ cup, 125 ml	4625	1105

FISH AND SEAFOOD

CANNED FISH

	kJ	Cals
Anchovies, in oil, drained, 1, 5 g	85	20
Crabmeat, in brine, 100 g	225	54
Drained, 100 g	255	60
Herrings, average in various sauces, 100 g	710	170
Mussels, smoked, in oil, drained, ⅕ can, 20 g	160	39
Oysters, smoked, in oil, drained, ⅕ can, 20 g	175	42
Salmon, Australian, in brine, 100 g	645	154
Drained, 100 g	730	174
Pink, in brine, 100 g	545	130
Drained	615	146
Red, in brine, 100 g	720	172
Drained	815	194
Sardines, in oil, 100 g	1280	305
Drained, 80 g	760	180
Tuna, in brine, 100 g	460	109
Drained, 100 g	520	123
Tuna, in oil, 100 g	1210	288
Drained, 100 g	920	220

Brand Names

ADMIRAL (per 100 g)	kJ	Cals
Anchovies flat	760	180
rolled	665	160
Clams, baby	350	83
Crab meat	255	61
Herring fillets in assorted sauces	715	170
Mackerel in brine	710	169
Mackerel sgombri in oil	765	183
Oysters, smoked	860	205
Mussels, smoked	810	193
Prawns, peeled	330	79
Sardines in oil	950	227
In tomato sauce	775	185
Seafood mix	480	115
Kipper fillets in brine	940	225
ALLY		
Salmon, pink, 100 g	670	160
Sardines in oil, 75 g	625	150
In tomato sauce, 80 g	730	173

GREENSEAS (per 100 g)	kJ	Cals
Frelish	605	145
Prepared as patties	850	203
Salmon, Australian	735	176
Chunks in brine	735	176
Tuna in brine	370	88
In oil	1690	404
In spring water	370	88
Chunk style, salt reduced	370	88
Sandwich	850	203

JOHN WEST	kJ	Cals
Anchovies, 18 g	170	41
Herrings in tomato sauce, 45 g	360	88
Kipper fillets, 65 g	620	148
Mackerel fillets in brine, 60 g	380	91
Mussels, smoked, 80 g	685	164
Oysters, smoked, 100 g	550	130
Pilchards in tomato sauce, 80 g	465	114
Salmon, red, 105 g	795	177
Med. red	705	168
Pink, in brine, 105 g	685	163
Tuna, in brine, 95 g	455	109
In oil, 103 g	890	212

KING OSCAR	kJ	Cals
Kipper fillets in natural juices, 200 g	1455	347
Herrings in tomato sauce, 170 g	1460	350
Sardines in oil, 100 g	1540	368

SAFCOL (per 100 g)	kJ	Cals
Mussels, smoked	765	183
Oysters, smoked	950	227
Salmon, Australian	805	192
Pink	630	150
Red	775	185
Silver	535	128
Sardines in tomato sauce	455	108
In vegetable oil	645	154
Tuna in brine	470	112
In oil	910	217
Sandwich	885	211

FISH DISHES

(per serve)	kJ	Cals
Fish and chips, average	2350	560
Fish mornay, 1 cup, 200 g	1100	265
Fish pie, 200 g	1880	450
Lobster mornay, ½ lobster	1660	400
Lobster thermidor, ½ lobster	1750	420
Prawn cocktail, 1 serve	415	100
With seafood cocktail sauce	770	185
Oysters Kilpatrick, 12	420	100
Oysters mornay, 12	470	110
Smoked fish mousse, 150 g	1100	265
Sole meunière, 1 fish	1995	480

FRESH FISH

(edible portion — 100 g)	kJ	Cals
Barramundi, raw	410	100
Steamed, poached, grilled	460	110
Crumbed, battered, fried	850	205
Bream, raw	520	124
Steamed, poached, grilled	580	140
Crumbed, battered, fried	970	230
Cod, smoked	355	85
Steamed, poached	400	95
Flake, raw	445	106
Steamed, poached, grilled	525	125
Crumbed, battered, fried	745	177
Flathead, fillet, raw	395	94
Steamed, poached, grilled	485	115
Crumbed, battered, fried	955	227
Flounder, raw	380	90
Steamed, poached, grilled	410	100
Crumbed, battered, fried	720	170
Gemfish, fillet, raw	805	192
Steamed, poached, grilled	940	225
Crumbed, battered, fried	1160	276
Jewfish, raw	325	80
Steamed, poached, grilled	380	90

	kJ	Cals
John Dory, raw	380	90
Steamed, poached, grilled	405	95
Crumbed, battered, fried	720	170
Herring, raw	500	120
Steamed, poached, grilled	550	130
Crumbed, battered, fried	790	190
Mackerel, raw	820	195
Steamed, poached, grilled	960	230
Crumbed, battered, fried	1220	290
Morwong, raw	545	130
Steamed, poached, grilled	530	125
Crumbed, battered, fried	835	200
Mullet, raw	550	130
Steamed, poached, grilled	560	135
Crumbed, battered, fried	1230	293
Mulloway, raw	435	104
Steamed, poached, grilled	540	130
Crumbed, battered, fried	800	190
Perch, raw	405	95
Steamed, poached, grilled	510	120
Crumbed, battered, fried	830	200
Salmon, raw	500	120
Steamed, poached, grilled	590	140

	kJ	Cals
Crumbed, battered, fried	810	195
Shark, see **flake**		
Sole, raw	380	90
Steamed, poached, grilled	410	100
Crumbed, battered, fried	720	170
Snapper, fillets, raw	405	96
Steamed, poached, grilled	510	120
Crumbed, battered, fried	835	200
Trout, raw	830	200
Steamed, poached, grilled	960	230
Crumbed, battered, fried	1120	270
Tuna, raw	450	110
Steamed, poached, grilled	510	120
Crumbed, battered, fried	830	200
Whiting, fillets, raw	360	85
Steamed, poached, grilled	435	105
Crumbed, battered, fried	1310	312

FROZEN FISH DINNERS

BIRDS EYE
(per 100 g)

	kJ	Cals
Battered crisps	740	176
Fish cakes	810	193

	kJ	Cals
Fish fillets in cheese sauce	470	112
Fish fingers	920	220
Whiting fillets	395	94
Fish with rice		
Fish Hollandaise with rice	510	122
Prawn scampi in garlic butter sauce with rice	505	120
Prawn fettuccini alfredo	375	89
Ovenfry		
Fish and chips, 100 g fish, 100 g chips	1665	397
Fish cakes	920	220
Fish portions	810	194
Crumbed	935	223
Lemon	880	210
Wholemeal	895	214
Junior, battered	810	194
Crumbed	935	223
Southern Blue whiting fillets	985	235
Microwiz crumbed fish fillets	865	206

I & J
Fish in sauce
(per 200 g serve)

	kJ	Cals
Cheese	610	145
Parsley	640	153
Lemon	835	200
Seafood	530	127
Fish fingers		
(per individual serving)		
Standard	195	46
Chunky	250	60
Tasty	200	47

	kJ	Cals
Sea shanties, 100 g	960	230
Sea cakes, 100 g	535	152
Tuna, 100 g	535	152

OTHER SEAFOOD

	kJ	Cals
Abalone, raw, 100 g	390	95
fried	570	135
Calamari (squid), raw, 100 g	330	80
Crumbed, fried, 5 rings	765	185
Clams, 6, meat only, steamed	350	85
Crab, fresh, meat only, 100 g	440	25
Crayfish/lobster, whole, per 100 g	410	97
Moreton Bay Bugs, meat only, 100 g	385	90
Mussels, 12 fresh, 100 g	360	85
Oysters, 12 fresh in shell	260	60
Prawns, king, cooked, 4 whole, 100 g	370	88
Prawns, school, cooked, 10 whole, 100 g	320	74
Prawn cocktail, 100 g	510	120
Scallops, uncooked, 12, 100 g	225	53
5 crumbed, battered, 100 g	440	105
Scampi, meat only, 100 g	200	50
Yabbies, meat only, 100 g	190	45

SMOKED FISH

(Per 100 g)	kJ	Cals
Cod	355	85
Eel	1100	265
Salmon	560	135
Trout	530	125

Level of Omega-3-EPA in certain fish

Eating several meals of fish per week may be beneficial to the cardiovascular system. Fish oils contain omega-3 eicosapentaenoic acid (EPA) oils that reduce risk of blood clots and atherosclerosis.

Although the fish contain significant amounts of cholesterol, the effect on blood cholesterol levels seems to be neutralised by the effect of omega-3. The high-fat fish contain more omega-3.

High
Canned mackerel, sardines, tuna, pink and red salmon.
Medium
Mullet, ocean perch, pilchards, trout, yellowtail.
Fair
Australian salmon, gemfish, whiting, flake, snapper, shellfish.

CANNED FRUIT

Weights given are with liquid drained	kJ	Cals
Apple, no added sugar, 100 g	155	36
Apricots, artificially sweetened, 100 g	100	24
In pear juice, 100 g	170	41
In syrup, 100 g	210	50
Blueberries, in syrup, 100 g	290	69
Cherries, in syrup, 100 g	295	70
Fruit salad, artificially sweetened, 100 g	125	30
In pear juice, 100 g	175	42
In syrup, 100 g	205	48
Fruit salad, tropical, heavy syrup, 100 g	330	78
In pineapple juice, 100 g	205	48
Lychees, in syrup, 100 g	290	69
Mandarin, in syrup, 100 g	245	58
Peaches, artificially sweetened, 100 g	105	25
In pear juice, 100 g	170	40
In syrup, 100 g	210	50
Pears, artificially sweetened, 100 g	110	26
In pear juice, 100 g	180	42
In syrup, 100 g	245	59
Pineapple, heavy syrup, 100 g	350	83

	kJ	Cals
In pineapple juice, 100 g	190	45
Plums, in syrup, 100 g	370	88
Raspberries, in syrup, 100 g	295	70
Strawberries, in syrup, 100 g	325	77

Brand Names

(per 100 g, liquid not drained)

ARDMONA/ GOULBURN VALLEY

Apricot halves, in light syrup	240	57
In natural juice	190	45
In water	120	28
Fruit salad, in light syrup	220	52
In natural juice	175	42
In water	140	33
Peach slices, in !ight syrup	230	55
In natural juice	180	43
In water	110	26
Halves, in light syrup	230	55
In natural juice	180	43
In water	110	26
Pear halves, in light syrup	235	56
In natural juice	180	43
In water	150	35

	kJ	Cals
Slices, in light syrup	235	56
Whole, in light syrup	235	56
Plums, whole, in light syrup	355	85
Two fruits, in light syrup	230	55
In natural juice	180	43
In water	135	32
Pie filling, apple	190	45

JOHN WEST

	kJ	Cals
Blackberries in syrup	255	61
Blueberries in syrup	290	70
Boysenberries in syrup	370	88
Cherries, black in syrup	265	64
Grapefruit in syrup	265	64
Lychees	290	69
Mandarins in syrup	215	51
Mango, pulp	455	109
Slices	330	70
Passionfruit pulp	365	87
Raspberries in syrup	370	88
Strawberries in syrup	345	82

WEIGHT WATCHERS

	kJ	Cals
Apricot halves	125	30
Peach slices	125	30
Pear halves	135	32
Two fruits	130	31

DRIED FRUIT

	kJ	Cals
Apples, 8 pieces, 30 g	330	80
Apricots, 5 pieces, 30 g	245	60
Banana chips, ¼ cup, 30 g	340	80
Cherries, glace, 5 whole, 30 g	420	100
Currants, ¼ cup, 50 g	560	133

	kJ	Cals
Dates, 4 pitted, 5 unpitted, 30 g	340	81
Figs, 2 pieces, 30 g	290	69
Fruit medley, ¼ cup, 30 g	340	81
Fruit mince, ⅔ cup, 100 g	1255	300
Fruit salad, ¼ cup, 30 g	340	81
Ginger, glace, ¼ cup, 30 g	420	100
Mixed fruit, ½ cup, 60 g	670	160
Mixed peel, ¼ cup, 30 g	400	95
Peaches, 3 pieces, 30 g	330	79
Pears, 3 pieces, 30 g	340	81
Prunes, 4 unpitted, 30 g	235	56
Raisins, ¼ cup, 30 g	365	87
Sultanas, ¼ cup, 30 g	385	91

FRESH FRUIT

Weights given are for the whole fruit as purchased

	kJ	Cals
Apple, average, 1 whole, small, 100 g	190	45
1 medium, 150 g	285	68
1 large, 200 g	380	90
Delicious, 100 g	210	50
Golden delicious, 100 g	170	40
Granny Smith, 100 g	170	40
Jonathan, 100 g	190	46
Apricots, average, 1 whole, medium, 40 g	60	14

	kJ	Cals		kJ	Cals
Avocado, ½ average, 100 g	660	157	Per grape, average	10	2
Babaco, ⅛ average, 100 g	80	20	Black muscatel, 100 g	330	78
Banana, peeled, 1 small, 70 g	165	40	Cornichon, 100 g	235	56
1 medium, 100 g	235	55	Sultana, 100 g	250	60
1 large, 170 g	395	95	Waltham cross, 100 g	255	60
Banana, 1 small sugar type, 60 g	175	41	Guava, 1 small, 100 g	100	24
Berries, average all types, ½ cup, 80 g	120	30	Honeydew melon, ⅛ small, 100 g	90	21
			1 cup cubes/balls, 150 g	130	30
Cantaloupe, ¼ medium, 250 g (150 g flesh)	140	33	Jackfruit, ⅛ average, 100 g	325	77
Carambola, 1 medium, 100 g	230	55	Kiwifruit, 1 small, 50 g	100	24
Cherries, 1 medium, 5 g	10	3	1 large, 80 g	165	40
20 medium, 100 g	225	53	Lemon, ½ average, 50 g	50	11
Cranberries, ½ cup, 100 g	65	16	Lime, 1 average, 50 g	45	11
			Loganberries, 100 g	75	18
Cumquat, 1 average, 8 g	20	5	Loquat, 1 medium, 25 g	20	4
Currants, average, small bunch, 100 g	120	30	Lychee, 1 average, 20 g	40	10
			Mandarin, 1 small, 40 g	65	16
Custard apple, ¼ medium, 100 g	220	52	1 medium, 60 g	100	23
			1 large, 90 g	145	35
Elderberries, 100 g	300	70	Mango, 1 average, 200 g	295	70
Feijoa, 1 medium, 100 g	50	12	1 large, 300 g	445	107
Fig, 1 large, 80 g	135	32	Melons, average, per 150 g flesh only	140	35
Fruit salad, average, ½ cup, 100 g	220	55	Mulberries, ¾ cup, 100 g	120	29
Gooseberries, ½ punnet, 80 g	90	22	Nashi fruit, 1 medium, 150 g	250	60
Grapefruit, ½ medium, 150 g	110	26	Nectarine, 1 small, 50 g	75	18
½ large, 200 g	150	35	1 average, 80 g	115	28
			1 large, 120 g	175	42
Grapes, average, small bunch, 100 g	255	61	Olives, black fresh, 1 medium, 5 g	35	8

	kJ	Cals
Black in brine, 1 medium, 7 g	50	12
Green fresh, 1 medium, 5 g	10	2
Green in brine, 1 medium, 7 g	15	4
Stuffed, 1 medium, 5 g	25	6
Orange, average, small, whole, 150 g	155	37
1 medium, whole, 200 g	210	49
1 large, whole, 300 g	310	74
Passionfruit, 1 small, 50 g	40	9
Pawpaw, ¼ small, 100 g	85	20
¼ large, 250 g	215	50
Peach, 1 small, 80 g	105	25
1 medium, 100 g	130	30
1 large, 200 g	265	63
Pear, average, 1 small, 120 g	215	52
1 medium, 150 g	270	64
1 large, 200 g	360	85
Pepino, 100 g	85	20
Persimmon, 1 medium, 100 g	190	46
Pineapple, ⅛ average, 225 g	240	57
1 slice, 2 cm, peeled, 90 g	140	34
Plum, average, 1 small, 50 g	75	17
1 medium, 90 g	130	31
1 large, 150 g	220	52
Pomegranate, ½ medium, 200 g	320	75

	kJ	Cals
Prickly pear, 1 medium, 100 g	130	31
Quince, 1 medium, 250 g	430	102
Rambutan, 1 average, 35 g	40	9
Raspberries, ⅔ cup, 100 g	105	25
Rhubarb, 1 stalk, 100 g	75	18
Rockmelon, ¼ small, 150 g (100 g flesh)	90	22
¼ medium, 250 g (150 g flesh)	140	33
¼ large, 350 g, (230 g flesh)	210	50
Starfruit, 1 medium, 100 g	230	55
Strawberries, 2 medium/1 large, 20 g	15	4
1 punnet, 20 medium, 170 g	135	32
Tamarillo, 1 medium, 75 g	85	20
Tangelo, 1 small, 100 g	155	37
1 medium, 150 g	235	56
1 large, 200 g	310	75
Watermelon, ½ slice, 3 cm, 200 g	190	46

STEWED FRUIT

	kJ	Cals
Average, apple/apricot/ pears, plums, average, ½ cup, 100 g, stewed with sugar	480	115
Stewed with no sugar	380	90

For a product to be called 'ice-cream', it must contain a minimum proportion of dairy products and its fat content will be greater than 10%. Ice confections contain a lower proportion of dairy products

	kJ	Cals
Icecream cone,		
1 single	80	18
1 double	110	25
1 cup	95	20
Sugar cone	150	35
Wafer, single	40	10
Waffle cone	350	85
Ice confection, vanilla		
1 scoop 100 ml, 50 g	365	85
1 litre	3650	873
2 litres	7300	1746
Icecream, vanilla,		
100 ml, 50 g	415	100
Soft serve, average, 1 cone (Mr Whippy, Wendy's, Dairy Frost, Dairy Queen etc.)	380	90

Brand Names

EVEREST

	kJ	Cals
Cassata, 1 serve	1140	273
Tartufo, 1 serve	950	227

	kJ	Cals
Gelati, average fruit flavour, 1 serve, 80 g	360	86
Chocolate/nougat, 1 serve, 80 g	510	122

NESTLÉ

	kJ	Cals
Cascade, 125 ml	760	180
Nougat, ⅛ whole, 63 g	590	140
Symphony, average all flavours, 125 ml portion	1100	263
Truffle, 125 ml portion	605	145

NORCO
(per 50 g scoop)

	kJ	Cals
Frozen dessert, low cholesterol	395	95
Ice confection, milk, average	370	88
Ice cream	425	100

NORGEN VAAS

	kJ	Cals
Single scoop, average	560	134
Home pack, 500 ml	3400	815
Vaaz bar	335	80

OAK

	kJ	Cals
Ice cream, 1 scoop, 100 ml, 50 g	840	200

PAULS
(per 50 g scoop, 100 ml)

	kJ	Cals
Dessert whip	705	170
Extra cream, vanilla/vanilla slices	420	100
Double choc chip	455	109

	kJ	Cals
Butterscotch brickle	465	110
Choc caramel swirl	415	99
Peppermint choc		
Mint chip	460	110
Mocha fudge	475	113

PETERS
(per 50 g scoop, 100 ml)

	kJ	Cals
Arctic delicacy, vanilla		
francaise	500	120
Chocolate mousse		
supreme	540	129
Cafe macadamia	530	126
Carbohydrate modified	270	65
light, vanilla	250	60
Apricot	275	57
Strawberry	290	68
Natural, vanilla/vanilla		
slices	415	99
Vanilla with apricots	405	80
Vanilla with		
strawberry	430	103
Vanilla with fruit		
salad	410	98
Original, vanilla	400	95
Neapolitan	405	97
Caramel swirl	405	97
Vanilla choc chip	460	110
Party cake	410	98
Royal, vanilla	440	105
Chocolate	450	107
Sorbet & cream,		
raspberry	310	74
Strawberry and		
peach	305	72
Standard, vanilla	410	98
Neapolitan	410	98
Caramel swirl	410	98

	kJ	Cals
Choc chip	470	112
Chocolate	420	100
Sundae twist	405	97

SARA LEE
(per 50 g scoop, 100 ml)

	kJ	Cals
Vanilla	505	120
Chocolate	485	115
Apricot	430	103
Strawberry and cream	420	100
Peach and mango	405	97
Honey and pecan	455	108

STREETS
(per 100 ml)

	kJ	Cals
All natural vanilla	405	97
Cal control	195	46
Quality favourite,		
Chocolate	370	89
Neapolitan	375	90
Vanilla	385	92
Super saver, neapolitan	400	95
Vanilla	400	95
Vanilla slice	400	95
Blue Ribbon		
Blue ribbon light	350	84
Chocolate	385	92
Strawberry	420	100
Toffee cream	465	111
Vanilla	385	92
Desserts		
Coffee walnut roll	385	92
Toffee roll	545	130
Viennetta cappuccino	555	133
Chocolate	550	132
Vanilla	505	121
Homer Hudson		
Butter pecan	1130	270
Chocolate rock	1125	269

	kJ	Cals
Hoboken crunch	1050	251
Rum and raisin	1005	241
Strawberry	930	222
Plumes		
After dinner mint	760	181
Apricot	660	158
Belgian chocolate	700	167
Irish cream	680	162
Pecan macadamia	775	185
Strawberry	650	155
Vanilla supreme	675	161
Walnut rum & raisin	730	175

SUNBURST REGENCY
(100 g per portion)

	kJ	Cals
Fruit tubes, orange	300	71
Orange/mango	300	71
Apple/blackcurrant	280	66
Apple/cherry	300	71
Ice drops (all flavours)	255	61
Sunny boy (all flavours)	175	41
Zooper doopers	350	83

WEIGHT WATCHERS
(per 50 g scoop, 100 ml)

	kJ	Cals
Ice confection	280	67

WHITE WINGS
(per stick)
Water Ice

	kJ	Cals
Kool pops	80	19
Funny face	180	43
All Natural Ice Blocks		
Orange	95	23
Orange/mango	95	23
Tropical	95	23
Space Food Sticks (for 2 sticks)		
Caramel	300	71
Chocolate	300	71

NOVELTIES

PETERS AND PAULS (per icecream)	kJ	Cals
Billabong, chocolate	410	98
Strawberry	410	98
Triple swirl	440	105
Banana (Barney)	410	98
Bubbleberry	550	130
Choc twist	590	141
Boska, vanilla	430	102
Chill stik	195	46
Choc o malt	730	174
Choc wedge, vanilla	755	180
Choc malt	770	183
Spearmint	755	180
White wedge	820	196
Crazy critters	325	77
Dixie cup	410	98
Donald duck	620	148
Drumstick, caramel/ vanilla	910	218
Mint chip/vanilla	850	203
Rocky road	880	211
Eskimo pie	860	206
Frisco, vanilla caramel	840	200
Frisco treats	485	115
Frosty fruit, tropical	320	76
Fruit Salad	280	66
Frozen yoghurt, apricot	535	127
Strawberry	535	127
Fruit de light	220	52
Icy-poles, raspberry	200	47
Lemonade	200	47
Pine orange	210	50
Cosmic blue	210	50
Mickey mouse	650	155

	kJ	Cals
Monaco bar	840	200
Skona	500	120
Split, raspberry	270	64
Pine orange	320	76
Lemon lime	350	83
Orange berry	360	86
Twister	870	208
Wild	890	213

STREETS
(per icecream)

	kJ	Cals
Bubble O'Bill	695	166
Calippo, lemon	505	121
Orange	510	121
Choc block, chocolate	860	206
Vanilla	900	216
Cool shark	230	55
Cornetto, ban passion	860	206
Blueberry	845	202
Choc mint	850	203
Chocolate	620	149
Strawberry	850	203
Vanilla	725	174
Dude food	385	92
Feast	1230	294
Fresh	715	171
Funster	340	81
Gaytime, coconut chocolate	905	216
Golden	860	206
Heart, mint	760	182
Vanilla	790	190
Hearts snack	410	99
Magnifico, caramel	960	230
Chocolate	970	232
Mighty choc, choc dip	480	115
Fruit	190	46
Milk	295	71

	kJ	Cals
Oz block, cola	230	56
Lemonade	230	55
Raspberry	230	55
O.J.	270	65
Paddle pop, banana	510	122
Caramel chocolate	560	133
Chocolate	650	155
Mint choc	555	133
Rainbow	510	122
Toffee-apple	550	132
Vanilla	515	124
Ripper dipper	235	56
Lemonade/pineapple	235	56
Pineapple/lime	235	56
Small cups	375	90
Splice, pine lime	395	94
Pineapple/passionfruit	380	91
Triple treat	935	224
Triples	220	53
Vienna chocolate	620	148
Winner	910	217
Yoghurt, fruit salad	440	105
Yoghurt, strawberry	470	112

TOFU

	kJ	Cals
Average 100 ml	625	150
Tofu supreme, fruit, 50 g, 100 ml scoop	625	150
Chocolate, 50 g, 100 ml scoop	640	155

MEAT AND MEAT PRODUCTS

BACON AND HAM

(per 100 g)	kJ	Cals
Bacon, 2 processed breakfast rashers, raw	400	95
3 fried	635	152
3 grilled	585	140
Bacon, 2 middle rashers, raw	1310	316
With fat removed	570	136
3 rashers, fried	1550	375
3 rashers, fat removed, fried	955	228
3 rashers, grilled	1340	323
3 rashers, fat removed, grilled	1000	240
Ham		
Ham, average	525	125
Leg	455	108
Shoulder	465	111
Steak, 1 small	520	124

	Fatty (as purchased)		Lean (all visible fat trimmed)	
BEEF	kJ	Cals	kJ	Cals
AVERAGE, ALL CUTS				
Small, 100 g raw, grilled	800	190	555	135
Medium, 150 g raw, grilled	1200	285	835	200
Large, 200 g raw, grilled	1600	380	1110	265
Very large, 250 g raw, grilled	2000	480	1390	330

BEEF CUTS (per 100 g)	Fatty (as purchased)		Lean (all visible fat trimmed)	
	kJ	Cals	kJ	Cals
Average, boneless	770	185	500	119
Blade steak, raw	745	178	545	129
Grilled	865	207	740	176
Brisket (pot roast), raw	835	200	395	94
Boiled	1300	310	890	213
Chuck steak, raw	650	156	455	109
Casseroled	1070	255	850	227
Corned beef, raw	625	150	410	98
Boiled	850	203	550	132
Fillet steak, raw	740	176	520	124
Grilled	975	233	820	195
Porterhouse (sirloin), raw	965	232	580	138
Grilled	1150	275	810	192
Rib steak, raw	1090	261	510	122
Grilled	1260	303	740	177
Round steak, raw	680	162	495	117
Grilled	850	203	740	177
Rump steak, raw	960	230	495	117
Grilled	1130	270	805	193
Scotch fillet, raw	800	191	555	133
Grilled	1070	257	830	200
Silverside, raw	780	187	460	110
Baked	970	232	745	177
Silverside, corned, raw	540	130	335	79
Boiled	850	203	545	130
Sirloin steak, raw	965	232	580	138
Grilled	1150	275	810	192
Skirt steak, raw	515	122	470	112
Casseroled	825	197	790	187
T-Bone, 120 g with bone, raw	965	232	580	138
120 g grilled	1150	275	807	192
Topside, raw	605	144	485	115
Roasted	800	190	635	152

LAMB

(per 100 g unless otherwise stated)	Fatty (as purchased)		Lean (all visible fat trimmed)	
	kJ	Cals	kJ	Cals
Average, raw, boneless	1200	289	500	119
Cooked	1390	335	810	193
Breast, rolled, stuffed, 2 thin slices	1190	286	—	—
Baked, 2 thin slices	1210	290	—	—
Chump chops, 120 g with bone, 1 raw	1180	282	590	140
Grilled, 1, with bone	1080	260	845	200
Crown roast, 130 g with bone, 3 ribs, raw	1190	287	600	143
140 g roasted, with bone	1200	290	810	193
Cutlets, 3 raw, 130 g, with bone	1190	287	600	143
Diced lamb, 1 cup, raw	730	175	470	111
Grilled	850	203	730	175
Leg of lamb, raw	730	175	470	111
Roasted, 2 slices	870	208	740	177
Loin chop, 2 raw, 130 g with bone	1190	285	600	143
120 g grilled, with bone	1200	287	810	194
Middle loin chops, 2 raw, 130 g with bone	1120	271	530	126
140 g grilled, with bone	1210	290	740	177
Neck chops (stewing), raw	1280	309	550	131
Stewed	1480	356	1060	253
Rack of lamb, 130 g, 3 ribs, raw	1190	287	600	143
3 ribs, roasted	925	220	490	117
Shank, 200 g, 1 raw	745	178	480	113
1 stewed	935	223	755	180
Shoulder, raw	840	202	480	114
2 slices, roasted	1030	248	780	186

LUNCHEON MEATS

(per 100 g)	kJ	Cals
Beef German	985	235
Berliner	945	225
Black pudding	1120	270
Bologna	1120	270
Brawn	910	220
Cabanossi	1520	365
Chicken Devon	985	235
Chicken roll	665	160
Devon/fritz	981	237
Garlic roll	1030	248
Ham & chicken roll	966	233
Ham sausage	1120	270
Kabana	1170	282
Luncheon roll	1220	290
Mortadella	1350	327
Pastrami	635	150
Polish sausage	1000	242
Pork sausage	1080	261
Strasbourg	1020	245

SALAMI

	kJ	Cals
Average	1800	431
Cabana	1250	300
Danish	1860	445
Hungarian	1780	426
Mettwurst	1790	428
Milano	1780	426
Pepperoni	1770	423
Polish	1750	420

MINCE

(raw, per 100 g)	kJ	Cals
Lean, e.g. topside (approx. 7% fat)	605	145
Average, e.g. spaghetti mince, (approx. 10% fat)	740	177
High fat, e.g. hamburger mince (approx. 15% fat)	925	220
Hamburger patties, small, 50 g	460	110
Medium, 75 g	690	165
Large, 100 g	925	220
Pork mince, average	1260	305

OFFAL

(per 100 g)	kJ	Cals
Beef heart	420	100
Kidney	370	87
Liver	705	169
Tail	1290	311
Tongue	835	200
Tripe	300	72
Tripe/cheese sauce, ½ cup	505	120
Haggis	1300	310
Lamb brains	505	121
Heart	510	122
Kidney	385	91
Liver	680	163
Tongue	835	201
Oxtail	1450	347
Sweetbreads	950	227
Veal heart	430	103
Kidney	450	108
Liver	570	137

MEAT AND MEAT PRODUCTS

PORK

(per 100 g unless otherwise stated)	Fatty (as purchased)		Lean (all visible fat trimmed)	
	kJ	Cals	kJ	Cals
Average, boneless, raw	1260	304	445	105
Cooked	1250	300	710	170
Butterfly steak, 1 average, raw	1110	268	450	107
Grilled	1090	262	680	163
Crackling, roasted, 20 g	400	95	—	—
Diced pork, 1 cup, raw	1310	317	450	106
Grilled	1440	346	760	181
Fillet, 1 raw	600	144	455	108
Roasted	710	170	550	132
Forequarter chop, 1 chop, 120 g				
with bone, raw	1310	317	450	106
Grilled, with bone	1095	262	420	100
Leg steak, raw	660	148	435	103
Grilled	720	172	655	157
Leg, raw	1170	283	430	101
2 slices, roasted	1420	340	720	172
Medallion steak, raw	1300	313	480	113
Grilled	1290	310	785	188
Midloin chops, 120 g with bone	1420	343	455	108
130 g, grilled	1520	365	730	175
Spare ribs, 3 ribs, raw	3700	885	1700	407
3 ribs, roasted	3000	720	1500	360

POULTRY AND GAME

CHICKEN

No skin

(per 100 g)	kJ	Cals
Chicken, average, raw	505	120
Roasted	785	188
Breast, raw	470	112
Battered and fried	980	235
Dry roasted	660	158
Drumstick, 2 average, raw	530	127
Battered and fried	1100	263
Dry roasted	875	210
Rotisseried	990	237

With skin

	kJ	Cals
Chicken, average, raw	800	190
Roasted	1030	245
Rotisseried	1010	242

	kJ	Cals
Breast average, raw	720	172
Battered and fried	1220	292
Dry roasted	915	218
Rotisseried	900	215
Drumstick, 2 average,		
raw	670	160
Battered and fried	1320	316
Dry roasted	1000	240
Rotisseried	1130	270

Other portions with skin

	kJ	Cals
Thigh, 1 average, raw,		
30 g	200	48
Battered and fried	400	95
Dry roasted	300	72
Rotisseried	340	80
Wing, 1 average,		
raw, 30 g	225	54
Battered and fried	500	120
Stuffing, ¼ cup, 50 g	400	95
Take-away chicken, see		
Take-Away Food		
Ready prepared meals,		
see **Canned,**		
Frozen and Packet		
Meals		

DUCK

	kJ	Cals
Duck, average, no fat or		
skin roasted	805	193
With fat and skin		
roasted	1405	336

GOOSE

	kJ	Cals
Goose, average, no fat or		
skin roasted	950	227
With fat and skin		
roasted	1850	443

TURKEY

	kJ	Cals
Turkey, hindquarter/		
breast, no fat or		
skin, roasted	720	172
With fat and skin,		
roasted	1010	242
TEGEL, breast, sliced,		
cooked	460	110
Hindquarter, basted, raw	700	168
Whole, basted, raw	615	147
Cooked	850	203
Deli-carve, cooked	500	120
Easy-carve buffe,		
basted, raw	610	146
Oven roasted breast		
roll, cooked	475	113
Buffe, with skin,		
cooked	655	156
Ready to roast breast		
roll, raw	425	102
Cooked	495	118
Smoked breast roll	450	107
Turkey hamwich	425	101
Turkey pastrami	460	110
Turkey salami	480	115

RABBIT

	kJ	Cals
Rabbit, average with		
bone, raw	520	124
Baked, with bone	600	145
Casseroled, 1 cup	650	155

MEAT AND MEAT PRODUCTS

SAUSAGES

	kJ	Cals
Beef, 1 thin 50 g, raw	365	87
Grilled	285	68
Fried	300	72
Beef, 1 thick 80 g, raw	545	130
Grilled	430	103
Fried	445	106
Beef and tomato/beef and chilli, 1 thin 50 g, raw	350	84
Grilled	290	70
Fried	300	72
Boerwors, 1 thick, 70 g, raw	530	127
Grilled	420	100
Fried	450	108
Chicken, 1 average, 50 g, raw	400	96
Grilled	295	70
Fried	320	77
Frankfurt, 1 average 40 g, boiled	435	104
Fried	510	122
Cocktail, 1 average 10 g, boiled	145	34
Lamb and herb, 1 average 60 g, raw	400	95
Grilled	300	72
Fried	320	77
Pork, 1 thin 50 g, raw	360	86
Grilled	280	67
Fried	290	70
Pork, 1 thick 80 g, raw	540	130
Grilled	420	100
Fried	440	105

	kJ	Cals
Saveloy, 1 average 70 g, boiled	755	180
Fried	835	200
Vienna, 125 g, plain	370	90
Fried	450	108

VEAL

(per 100 g)	Fatty (as purchased)		Lean (all visible fat trimmed)	
	kJ	Cals	kJ	Cals
Average, boneless, raw	505	120	435	103
Cooked	670	160	625	150
Forequarter, 120 g with bone, raw	570	136	455	107
½ cup casseroled	785	188	725	173
Leg Steak, raw	490	116	460	109
Fried	670	160	645	155
Leg, raw	415	98	370	87
2 slices roasted	595	142	575	138
Loin chops, 140 g with bone, raw	545	130	440	104
150 g grilled	675	160	610	146
Schnitzel, raw	490	116	460	109
Grilled	600	145	580	140
1 small crumbed, raw, 100 g	640	154	610	146
Fried	1360	325	1330	318
1 large crumbed, raw, 200 g	1280	300	1220	292
Fried	2030	485	1970	470
Shank, no bone, raw	450	105	380	90
½ cup, stewed	740	177	610	146
Shoulder steak, raw	540	129	480	113
Grilled	645	155	610	145

MISCELLANEOUS COOKING PRODUCTS

ARTIFICIAL SWEETENERS

	kJ	Cals
Equal (Nutrasweet), 1 tablet	0	0
1 sachet (= 2 tsp sugar)	16	4
Saccharin, 1 tablet	0	0
1 sachet (= 2 tsp sugar)	16	4

BAKING PRODUCTS

	kJ	Cals
Baking powder, 1 tsp, 3 g	15	4
Baking soda, 1 tsp, 3 g	0	0
Cake decorations		
100s & 1000s, 1tsp	40	10
Chocolate sprinkles, 1 tsp	50	12
Flavoured extracts, per tsp		
Brandy/rum essence	60	14
Lemon/peppermint, imitation	60	14
Pure	120	30
Vanilla, imitation	15	4
Pure	50	12
Gelatine 1 tsp, 3 g	40	10
1 sachet, 10 g	125	30
Marzipan, 30 g	560	135
Yeast, compressed, 10 g	40	10
Dried, 10 g	90	22

COATING MIXES

CONTINENTAL	kJ	Cals
Perfection microwave meat coatings, 20 g		
Country herb chicken	380	91
Honey and sesame chicken	300	72
Pepper steak	260	61
Satay chicken	300	72
Spicy Chinese	250	59
Steak diane	300	72
TANDACO (per 75 g pack)		
Chicken, seasoned	950	230
Southern fried	1045	250
Fish, lightly seasoned	1025	245
Schnitzel	1025	245

DRINKING POWDERS

	kJ	Cals
Cocoa powder, per tsp	65	15
Coffee powder, instant, per tsp	20	5
Malted milk powder, per tsp	70	16
Milo, per tsp	80	19
Milk powder, whole per tbsp	405	97
Milk powder, skim per tbsp	295	70

MARINADES, VINEGAR

	kJ	Cals
Teryaki sauce, 1 tbsp, 20 ml	70	17
Vinegar, 1 tbsp, 20 ml	15	4
LAWRY'S (per packet, prepared)		
Beef marinade	205	50
Chicken marinade	195	47
Lamb marinade	255	60
Pork marinade	330	80

SALT, PEPPER, HERBS

Salt, lite salt	0	0
Garlic/celery salt, 1 tsp, 3 g	15	4
Seasoned salt, 1 tsp, 3 g	15	3
Pepper, ground, 1 tsp	25	6
Seasoned, 1 tsp	40	9
Curry powder, 1 tsp	30	7
Garlic powder, 1 tsp	40	10
Mixed herbs, 1 tsp	10	3
Mustard, dried, 1 tsp	45	11
Nutmeg, 1 tsp	45	11
Parsley, dried, 1 tsp	10	3

STOCK CUBES

MAGGI (per cube)		
Bacon	40	10
Beef	25	6
Chicken	40	10
Onion	45	11

SUGARS AND SYRUPS

	kJ	Cals
Golden syrup, 1 tbsp, 25 g	300	72
Honey, 1 tsp, 6 g	85	20
1 tbsp, 25 g	330	79
Malt extract syrup, 1 tbsp, 25 g	330	79
Molasses, light, 1 tbsp, 25 g	260	62
Sugar, brown, 1 tsp	65	16
1 tbsp	260	62
½ cup, 90 g	1360	325
Castor, ½ cup, 125 g	2000	480
Icing, ½ cup, 75 g	1200	290
Raw, 1 tsp	65	16
½ cup, 100 g	1600	385
Sugar, white, 1 tsp (level)	65	16
Rounded tsp (1½ level)	100	24
1 tbsp	270	65
1 cube	100	24
½ cup, 125 g	2000	480
Sugar cane juice, 1 tbsp	65	16
½ cup, 125 g	500	120

PULSES AND BEANS

(per ½ cup, 100 g)	kJ	Cals
Broad beans, fresh shelled	440	105
Butter beans, dry	1160	278
Cooked	405	97
Black eye, borlotti, dry	1350	323
Cooked	420	100
Cannellini beans, dry	1060	255
Cooked	400	96
Carob bean powder, dry	1600	383
Cooked	415	100
Chick peas/red/navy/ white beans, dry	1100	263
Cooked	450	108
Haricot beans, dry	1050	150
Cooked	395	95
Lentils, dry	1090	260
Cooked	420	100
Lima beans, dry	1090	260
Cooked	520	124
Canned	470	112
Mixed beans, 3 bean mix, canned	445	107
Mung beans, dry	990	237
Cooked	445	105
Red kidney beans, dry	1060	254
Cooked	310	75
Canned	360	85
Soybeans, dry	1490	355
Cooked/canned	450	108
Split peas, dry	1240	297
Cooked	450	108

BAKED BEANS

(per ½ cup, 100 g)	kJ	Cals
Average, in tomato sauce	345	82
FARMLAND, tomato sauce	400	95
HEINZ		
Baked beans in BBQ sauce	470	112
In ham sauce	465	111
Salt reduced	385	92
In tomato sauce	385	92
Viva La Beanz		
Boston	525	125
Chilli	450	108
Curried	500	119
Spicy Italian	425	101
PMU, tomato sauce	200	50
SPC, tomato sauce	390	93

PULSES AND BEANS

SALADS AND SALAD DRESSINGS

SALADS

(per 100 g)	kJ	Cals
HEINZ		
(canned)		
Hawaiian	490	117
Garden bean	335	80
Potato	390	93
Traditional vegetable	300	71
KENTUCKY FRIED CHICKEN		
(per small tub)		
Bean salad	565	135
Coleslaw	400	95
Potato salad	560	134
MASTER FOODS		
(canned)		
Bean 'n' corn	405	96
Mixed beans	225	53
Mixed vegetables	185	44
Potato	480	115
Rice	300	71
Tropical	360	86
Zucchini	170	40
WHITE WINGS		
(½ cup serve, prepared)		
Salad plus		
Creamy macaroni	1010	240
Creamy twists	1010	240
French vinaigrette	565	135
Italian vinaigrette	565	135
Khorma curry	1010	240
Rice salad	710	169

SALAD DRESSINGS

FOUNTAIN SALAD MAGIC (per 30 ml)	kJ	Cals
No Cholesterol Low Oil		
Coleslaw dressing	320	76
Sour cream and chives	305	73
Thousand island	275	65
No Oil		
French	40	9
With garlic	45	10
Herb and garlic	50	11
Italian	80	19
Lemon with ginger	75	18
White wine vinaigrette	70	17
Mayonnaise,		
Cholesterol free, 1 tbsp		
20 g	180	43
Natural low oil, 1 tbsp		
20 g	265	63
HEINZ		
(per 1 tbsp, 20 g)		
English style salad		
cream	275	65
Mayonnaise	300	72
KRAFT		
(per tbsp, 20 g)		
Coleslaw	355	85
Creamy Caesar	295	70
French	190	45
French and herb	150	36
French and mustard		
seed	185	44

	kJ	Cals
Herb and garlic	220	52
Italian	240	57
Ranch potato and pasta	330	79
Thousand island	330	79
Light		
Coleslaw	45	10
French	30	7
Herb and garlic	5	1
Italian	5	1
Thousand island	150	36
Cholesterol free		
Coleslaw	170	40
French	30	7
French and herb	15	3
Italian	10	2
Canola		
French	190	45
Mayonnaise	280	67
Canola	280	67
Light	170	40
Free	140	33

LEISURE
(per 100 g)

	kJ	Cals
Chive and parsley	1050	250
Garlic and herbs	1050	250
Olive oil and lemon	1025	245
Traditional	1000	240

PAUL NEWMANS
(per 100 g)

	kJ	Cals
Salad dressing	1530	366
Light Italian	1200	286

WEIGHT WATCHERS

	kJ	Cals
Mayonnaise, 1 tbsp, 20 g	140	33

CHOOSING FATS AND OILS

• **Margarine** is manufactured from vegetable oils (which are liquid at room temperature) and treated through partial hydrogenation to make it spreadable at room temperature. Hydrogenation partially saturates the oil which negates some of the health benefits of the polyunsaturated oil. In addition, a side effect of the hydrogenation is to leave some byproducts which may increase blood cholesterol levels. **Use margarine in moderation.**

• **Vegetable oils** which are kept at high temperatures for deep frying, such as in many restaurants and fast food establishments, undergo chemical changes and produce materials which increase cardiovascular risk. **So avoid deep-fried foods, particularly from fast food outlets.**

• Where possible use polyunsaturated and monounsaturated oils instead of saturated fats.

• Use corn, sunflower seed, sesame seed, peanut and olive oils in preference to margarine.

SEEDS AND NUTS

NUTS

(per 30 g)	kJ	Cals
Almonds, shelled, approx. 25	730	175
Sugar coated	550	130
Chocolate coated	700	165
Beer nuts, approx. 30	720	170
Brazil, shelled, 8 medium	840	200
Cashews, roasted, approx. 15	785	185
Honey roasted	780	185
Chestnuts, approx. 5	205	50
Coconut, fresh	335	80
Dessicated, 4 tbsp	785	185
Milk, from nut, 100 ml	90	20
Cream	250	60
Hazelnuts, approx. 30	780	185
Macadamia nuts, approx. 12	905	215
Marzipan (almond paste)	505	120
Mixed salted nuts, approx. 20	780	185
Peanuts, raw, shelled, approx. 40	690	165
Raw, unshelled	540	130
Roasted in oil, shelled	750	180
Dry roasted, shelled	730	175
Honey roasted	670	160
Scorched peanuts, chocolate coated	675	160
Sugar coated	520	125
Pecans, shelled, approx. 25 halves	875	210
Pine nuts, ⅓ cup	865	205
Pistachio, shelled, approx. 30	695	165
Walnuts, shelled, approx. 20 halves	855	205

SEEDS

(per 1 tbsp, 30 g)	kJ	Cals
Caraway	245	60
Pumpkin seeds, dried	660	155
Safflower, hulled	695	165
Sesame, 2 tbsp	735	175
Sunflower, hulled	695	165
Tahini (seed paste)	785	185

SNACK FOODS

Average all brands	kJ	Cals
Corn chips, 25 g	520	125
50 g	1040	250
100 g	2080	500
Popcorn, plain, 2 cups,		
25 g	385	92
Sugar coated, 25 g	400	96
Microwave, 25 g	540	129
Potato chips, 25 g	550	132
50 g	1100	264
100 g	2200	528
Potato straws, 25 g	540	129
50 g	1080	258
Pretzels, 25 g	400	96
Soya chips/crisps, 25 g	100	24

Brand Names

(per 50 g pack)	kJ	Cals
Bacon rings, 25 g	520	124
Burger rings	1045	250
CCs corn chips,		
cheese	1050	251
French onion	1030	246
Mexican	1030	246
Natural	1060	253
Tangy barbeque	1030	246
Cheezels	1085	260
Chickadees	1015	243
Chik nix, 15 g	300	71
Firecrackers, 75 g	1610	385
French fries	1100	263
Golden dippers, 75 g	1410	337
Happy snax, 15 g	325	77

Lites lightly salted	kJ	Cals
potato chips	1105	264
Barbeque	1050	251
Cheese and onion	1070	255
Chicken	1100	263
Salt and vinegar	1090	260
Thin sliced	1000	239
Nobby's dry roasted		
peanuts	1305	312
Salted beer nuts	1290	308
Cashews	1265	302
Mixed nuts	1130	270
Peanuts	1320	315
Savoury roasted		
peanuts	1295	309
Noughts and crosses	1095	262
Ollos, 25 g	545	130
Pappadums, 75 g	1520	364
Planter's, beer nuts	1165	278
Dry roasted peanuts	1265	302
Cashews	1265	302
Exotic mix	1130	270
Honey roast cashews	1230	294
Peanuts	1275	305
Peanuts and		
cashews	1250	299
Lo-salt peanuts	1305	312
Lo-salt mixed nuts	1385	331
Macadamia	1585	379
Premium peanuts	1320	315
Samboy potato chips,		
barbeque	1120	268
Cheese and onion	1135	271
Chicken	1125	269

	kJ	Cals
Salt and vinegar	1120	268
Tomato sauce	1130	270
Seashells marinara, 75 g	1500	358
Smith's potato crisps,		
barbeque	1115	267
Chicken	1125	269
Less oil crinkle cut	1037	248
Original crinkle cut	1145	273
Salt and vinegar	1120	268
Sour cream and		
chives	1135	271
Tomato sauce	1130	270
Sticks lightly salted		
potato straws		
Salt and vinegar	1060	253
Tomato	1060	253
Twisties, cheese	1040	248
Chicken	1030	246

HEALTH BARS

EUROPE (per bar)

	kJ	Cals
Apricot coconut bar,		
50 g	655	156
Caramel chew, 30 g	565	135
Fruit nougat bar, 45 g	680	162
Ginger bar, 40 g	635	152
Honey log, 45 g	930	222
Jupiter caramel bar,		
30 g	590	141
Nut chew, 20 g	380	91
Peanut bar, 30 g	675	161
Peanut surprise bar,		
45 g	835	200
Peppermint truffle, 35 g	645	154
Raspberry chew, 20 g	385	92
Sesame bar, 45 g	845	202
Summer roll, 45 g	910	218

	kJ	Cals
SUN HEALTH BARS		
Almond and honey, 35 g	790	188
Apricot, 50 g	860	205
Cherry supreme, 25 g	430	103
Chewy sesame, 45 g	805	192
Hazelnut and honey,		
35 g	840	200
Macadamia and honey,		
35 g	900	215
Peanut and honey, 35 g	810	193
Sunflower and nut, 35 g	840	200
Tropical fruit, 50 g	770	184
Junior Range, per 25 g		
Apricot treat	475	113
Chewy muesli	430	103
Chewy peanut	445	106
Chewy sesame	445	106

MUESLI BARS

	kJ	Cals
CADBURY, muesli		
munch	960	230
GOLD CREST, fruit bars,		
average	600	144
Fruit and chocolate		
chip	625	150
Chocolate-coated		
bars	675	160
NO FRILLS, average,		
30 g bar	490	117
UNCLE TOBY'S,		
chocolate chip,		
average	565	135
Fruit, crunchy/chewy,		
average	520	124
Muesli wrapps,		
average	610	146

(prepared per instructions, 100 ml)

CAMPBELLS	kJ	Cals
All Natural		
Creamy asparagus	320	76
Broccoli	195	46
Carrot	225	54
Cauliflower	250	60
Corn	245	59
Chicken and corn	300	72
Potato and leek	250	60
Pumpkin	190	45
French onion	95	23
Garden mushroom	140	33
Tomato	115	27
Vegetable	150	36
Tomato and vegetable	105	25
Chunky		
Beef	280	67
Beef and mushroom	200	47
Beef and pasta	270	65
Chicken	245	59
Chicken and pasta	250	60
Ham and pea	360	86
Lamb	335	80
Minestrone	230	55
Stockpot	255	61
Vegetable	185	44
Red and white label		
Beef broth	45	10
Chicken broth	45	10
Chicken vegetable	110	26
Country vegetable	100	24
Cream of asparagus	270	65
Celery	215	51

	kJ	Cals
Chicken	235	56
Chicken and corn	225	54
Chicken and mushroom	280	67
Mushroom	260	62
Oyster	215	51
Minestrone	155	37
Old fashioned stockpot	135	32
Split pea with ham	270	65
Tomato	105	25
Vegetable	125	30
Vegetable beef	190	45
Salt reduced		
Cream of chicken	245	59
Mushroom	200	47
Tomato	80	19
Vegetable	125	30

CONTINENTAL	kJ	Cals
Cup-a-soup		
Chicken and vegetable	295	70
Noodle	185	44
Cream of celery	405	97
Chicken	220	52
Mushroom	460	109
Hearty beef	280	67
Pea and ham	485	116
Savoury vegetable	395	94
Spring vegetable	165	40
Tomato	460	110
Cup-a-soup special		
Asparagus with herb croutons	535	128

	kJ	Cals
Corn and chicken with croutons	590	141
Creamed vegetable	770	184
Dutch curry and rice	515	123
Hearty chicken	615	147
Seafood bisque	710	170
Spanish tomato	555	132
Vegetables and beef	435	104
Virginia pea and ham	620	148
Lots-a-noodles		
Beef	640	153
Chicken	620	148
Cream of chicken	685	164
Mild curry	620	148
Tomato	675	161
Vegetable	533	127
Slim-a-soup		
Beef and tomato	170	41
Chicken florentine	160	39
With wholemeal croutons	180	43
Garden, broccoli	190	46
Vegetables	135	34
Mushroom and chives	155	38
Oriental beef and vegetables	160	40
HEINZ		
Creamy condensed		
Asparagus	250	59
Celery	275	65
Chicken	305	73
Chicken asparagus	230	55
Chicken and mushroom	250	62
Chicken and corn	250	60
Curried chicken	320	76
Mushroom	280	67
Pumpkin	260	62

	kJ	Cals
Potato and leek	245	59
Seafood with lobster	260	62
Condensed		
Alphabet noodles in chicken soup	95	22
Beef broth	135	33
Chicken and vegetables	90	22
Dinosaurs in tomato soup	170	40
Minestrone	120	28
Mulligatawny	145	34
Pea with ham	205	49
Scotch broth	130	31
Tomato	125	30
Tomato and bacon	145	35
Tomato, salt reduced	125	30
Vegetable	135	32
Vegetable beef	105	25
Zesti tomato	140	34
International		
Indonesian curried vegetables	220	52
Mediterranean minestrone	170	40
Mexican bean	220	52
Tomato and basil	170	40
Main course		
Beef burgundy	190	45
Beef and mushroom stroganoff style	370	88
Chicken and corn	225	54
Chicken and pasta with vegetables	260	62
Chunky beef with vegetables	240	58
Ham and pea	180	42
Chicken	320	74

	kJ	Cals		kJ	Cals
Spring lamb	420	100	**WEIGHT WATCHERS**		
Soup for one			**Condensed**		
Beef and vegetables	170	40	Asparagus	160	38
Chicken noodle	160	38	Carrot and lentil	160	38
Creamy chicken	255	61	Chicken	95	23
Pumpkin	245	59	Country mushroom	170	41
Tomato	240	58	Tomato	95	23
Minestrone	180	43	Vegetable	90	21
Pea	220	53	**Instant Soups**		
P.M.U.			Chicken noodle	85	20
Chicken & vegetable	90	21	Garden vegetable	70	17
Chicken noodle and			Hearty beef	70	17
vegetable	70	17	Minestrone	80	19
Cream of chicken	85	20	Tomato & herb	75	18
Mushroom	105	25	**WHITE WINGS**		
Pea and ham	190	45	**Trim soup**		
Spring vegetable	75	18	Asparagus	165	40
Tomato	120	29	Beef	185	44
Tomato and bacon	150	36	Chicken	185	44
Vegetable beef	120	29	Chicken noodle	205	49
Wholesoups			Chicken and corn	170	41
Country stockpot	280	57	Curry and rice	170	41
Garden vegetable in			French onion	160	38
pureed pumpkin	190	45	Mild chicken curry	160	38
Golden corn	280	67	Mushroom	175	42
Meadow mushroom	230	55	Pea and ham	190	45
Tomato and lentil	295	71	Potato and leek	180	43
Winter vegetable	245	59	Sweet corn	170	41
MAGGI			Tomato	180	43
Asparagus	105	25	Vegetable	200	48
Chicken noodle	75	18			
Creme of chicken	110	26			
French onion	70	17			
Leek and potato	115	27			
Mushroom	130	31			
Spring vegetable	45	11			
Thick vegetable	110	26			

SOUPS

TAKE-AWAY FOOD

	kJ	Cals
Chicken		
Chicken nuggets, 6 average	1300	310
Chicken schnitzel	1700	405
Chicken schnitzel in sandwich	2585	615
Crumbed 1 portion, 140 g	1930	460
Rotisseried, ¼ chicken	1350	320
¼ chicken with stuffing	1555	370
Chips		
Chips, 1 bucket, 150 g	1545	368
Potato cakes, 1 average, 80 g	700	167
Potato gems, 150 g	1545	368
Hamburgers, hot dogs, Doner kebabs		
Hamburger, plain, 150 g	1400	334
Bacon, 170 g	1800	430
Cheese, 170 g	1830	436
Egg, 200g	1970	470
The lot, 300 g	2950	705
Doner kebab, 400 g	2400	575
Hot dog, 1 average	1350	323
with tomato sauce	1450	347
Fish and other seafoods		
Battered, deep fried, 150 g piece	1350	320
Calamari, crumbed, fried, 1 ring, 20 g	250	60

	kJ	Cals
Fish stick, fried, 25 g	150	36
Prawn, deep fried, 1 prawn, 30 g	330	79
Fried foods		
Battered saveloy, 1 average	1325	316
Chiko roll, 1 average, 190 g	1795	428
Dim sim, 1 average, 50 g, fried	465	110
Steamed	300	72
Spring roll, 1 large, 190 g	1905	454
1 small, 50 g	600	145
Pastries (1 average)		
Meat pie, 200 g	1894	450
Pastie, 200 g	2200	524
Sausage roll, 100 g	1200	285
Pasta (per entrée size serve)		
Cannelloni	1215	290
Lasagne	1088	260
Pasta, alfredo	1950	464
Bolognese	2100	500
Carbonara	2160	514
Matriciana	2350	560
Potatoes, baked (200 g potato with toppings)		
Potato, butter, cheese	1240	297
Butter, chilli	1280	306
Butter, baked beans	1020	244
Butter, sour cream, cheese	1520	365

	kJ	Cals
Butter, sour cream, cheese, coleslaw	1600	383
Sour cream, cheese, coleslaw	1300	310
Yoghurt, coleslaw	735	176
Sandwiches and rolls (Average per sandwich)		
Cheese	1170	280
Cheese and tomato	1175	280
Chicken, roast	1385	330
Corned beef	1300	310
Egg	1170	280
Ham	1300	310
Ham and cheese	1590	380
Salad	885	212
Tuna	1170	280
Extra fillings:		
Cheese	295	70
Lettuce	5	1
Tomato	10	2
Chutney/Pickles	30	7
Mayonnaise	85	20

Brand Names

HUNGRY JACK'S (per serve)	kJ	Cals
Burgers		
Bacon double cheeseburger	2105	503
Deluxe	2415	578
Great Aussie burger	2475	592
Grilled chicken burger	1730	406
Mini burger	1130	271
With cheese	1320	315
Chicken nuggets		
(4 pieces)	850	204
With plum sauce	955	228

	kJ	Cals
With sweet & sour	960	229
Whaler fish sandwich	1600	386
Whopper sandwich	2510	602
With bacon	2705	647
With cheese	2700	646
With egg	2640	632
Whopper junior sandwich	1445	346
With cheese	1630	390
Yumbo ham and cheese sandwich	1415	339
Apple pie	1005	240
Sundae, caramel	1030	246
Chocolate	1000	241
Strawberry	915	219
French fries (small)	950	226
Onion rings, 8–10	915	218
Shake chocolate	1160	277
Strawberry	1180	282

KENTUCKY FRIED CHICKEN (Fried chicken portions — per portion)	kJ	Cals
Average per 100 g portion, with bone	1300	310
Average per 100 g portion, no bone	1000	238
Breast	1100	262
Drumstick	660	157
Rib	855	204
Thigh	1190	283
Wing	610	145
Burgers, bacon and cheese chicken fillet, 1 average, 200 g	2140	511
Chicken fillet, 1 average, 170 g	1785	427

	kJ	Cals
Colonel	1195	286
Corn, 100 g	570	136
Kentucky **nuggets**, each, 20 g	165	40
Salads, coleslaw, 100 g tub	400	95
Potato/bean, 100 g tub	560	133
Mashed potato and gravy, small, approx 100 g	280	67
Gravy, per tub	1060	252

McDONALDS
Burgers, per item
	kJ	Cals
Big Mac	2500	597
Cheeseburger	1350	323
Fillet o' fish	1685	402
Junior burger	1170	279
Quarter pounder with cheese	2500	597
McFeast	2235	535

Chicken McNuggets
	kJ	Cals
6 nuggets	1360	325
9 nuggets	2035	487
20 nuggets	4525	1082
Barbeque sauce, per serve	210	51
Mild curry sauce, per serve	185	44
Sweet mustard sauce	235	56
Sweet and sour sauce	235	56

Fries
	kJ	Cals
Regular	855	205
Large	1375	329

Breakfasts
	kJ	Cals
Big breakfast	2575	616
Hash browns	760	181
McMuffin, bacon and egg	1490	356
Sausage	1415	338
Sausage with egg	1770	423
Scrambled eggs and English muffin	1520	364
English Muffin with Butter and jam	960	230
Hot cakes, butter and syrup	2150	514

Desserts
	kJ	Cals
Apple pie	1150	274
McDonaldland cookies	1215	291
Sundae, caramel	1050	251
Hot fudge	1115	266
Strawberry	1135	272

Drinks
	kJ	Cals
Coffee, white	105	25
black	10	2
Tea, white	50	12
black	—	—
Orange juice, regular	265	63
Large	440	105
Shakes, chocolate	1410	337
Strawberry	1505	360
Vanilla	1320	316

PIZZA HUT
Pan (per medium slice)
	kJ	Cals
Cheese	1090	260
Hawaiian	1225	293
Supreme	1435	343
Super supreme	1425	340

Thin 'n' crispy (per medium slice)
	kJ	Cals
Cheese	910	217
Hawaiian	1015	243
Supreme	1195	286
Super supreme	1215	290

VEGETABLES

DRIED VEGETABLES

(Deb, Dewcrisp, Surprise)	kJ	Cals
Beans, green, cooked, 50 g	60	15
Carrots, dry 15 g, cooked, 50 g	120	30
Corn, dry 15 g, cooked, 50 g	125	30
Mushrooms, dried 5 g, cooked 50 g	45	11
Peas, cooked, ½ cup, 60 g	116	28
Potatoes, mashed, 100 g	380	90
Vegetables, mixed, dry 15 g, cooked 50 g	125	30

FRESH, CANNED, FROZEN

Fresh vegetables as purchased

	kJ	Cals
Alfalfa, 1 punnet, 125 g	160	38
Artichoke, globe, 200 g	160	38
Jerusalem, 100 g	95	22
Canned, 100 g	70	16
Asparagus, 5 spears, 100 g	70	17
Canned, 5 spears, 100 g	70	17
Baked beans, canned, in sauce, 100 g	285	68
Bamboo shoots, canned, 100 g	35	8
Bean sprouts, 1 cup, 100 g	85	20
Beans, Broad, ½ cup, 100 g	175	41
Frozen, boiled, ½ cup, 100 g	245	59
Butter, ½ cup, 100 g	80	19
Green, French, ½ cup, 100 g	90	21
Canned, 100 g	100	24
Dried, boiled, 100 g	120	28
Frozen, boiled, 100 g	80	19
Purple, ½ cup, 100 g	120	28
Snake, ⅔ cup, 100 g	95	22
Beetroot, 1 small, 100 g	175	41
Canned, 6 slices, 2 whole baby, 100 g	170	40
Broccoli, 4–5 florets, 100 g	100	24
Frozen, boiled, 100 g	90	22
Brussel sprouts, 6 small, 100 g	70	17
Frozen, boiled, 100 g	150	36
Cabbage, Chinese, shredded 1 cup, 60 g	25	6
Green, shredded 1 cup, 60 g	45	10
Red, shredded 1 cup, 60 g	60	14

	kJ	Cals
Savoy, shredded		
1 cup, 60 g	45	10
Capsicum, green,		
1 small, 100 g	70	17
Red, 1 small, 100 g	105	25
Carrots, 5 baby, 2 small,		
1 medium, 100 g	105	25
1 large, 175 g	180	45
Grated, ½ cup, 60 g	60	15
Sticks, 10 g	10	2
Canned, 100 g	85	20
Frozen, boiled, 100 g	90	21
Cassava, white, peeled,		
100 g	660	160
Yellow, peeled, 100 g	550	130
Cauliflower, ½ cup,		
100 g	80	20
1 average, whole,		
20-cm diam.,		
1000 g	800	190
Frozen, boiled, 100 g	70	15
Celeriac, 100 g	120	30
Celery, 1 stalk, 60 g	30	7
Champignons, canned,		
100 g	65	15
Chard, ½ cup, 100 g	40	10
Chicory, 100 g	50	12
Chilli, 1 banana, 50 g	30	7
3 green, 50 g	40	10
3 red, 50 g	60	15
Chives, 2 tbsp chopped,		
20 g	20	5
Choko, ¼ medium,		
50 g	40	10
Coleslaw, canned,		
½ cup, 100 g	370	90
Collards, ½ cup, 100 g	170	40
Corn, see sweetcorn		

	kJ	Cals
Cucumber, average,		
4–5 slices, 50 g	15	5
1 whole, 400 g	135	35
Lebanese, 4–5 slices,		
50 g	25	6
Eggplant, 2 cm slice,		
50 g	35	8
Fried in oil/marg.,		
50 g	145	35
Endive, 50 g	20	5
Fennel, 50 g	40	10
Garlic, 1 clove, 3 g	10	2
Minced, John West		
jar, 1 tsp	25	6
Ginger, 1 tbsp grated,		
10 g	10	2
Crystallised,		
10 g piece	140	35
Ground, 1 tsp, 4 g	40	10
Gourd, wax, peeled,		
50 g	15	3
Horseradish, 20 g	40	10
Kale, ⅓ cup, 50 g	80	20
Kohlrabi, chopped,		
½ cup, 50 g	70	16
Leek, 1 bulb with 3 cm		
leaf, 50 g	55	13
Lettuce, common,		
2 leaves, 20 g	5	1
1 cup, shredded	5	1
Cos, 2 leaves, 30 g	20	5
Mignonette,		
2 leaves, 20 g	10	2
Lotus root, 50 g	100	25
Marrow, 100 g	70	17
Mustard greens,		
½ cup, 50 g	45	11
Mung bean sprouts, see		
bean sprouts		

	kJ	Cals
Mushroom, button, ½ cup, 50 g	50	12
Field, 3–4, 50 g	45	11
Oyster, ½ cup, 50 g	65	16
Canned, butter sauce, 100 g	115	27
Okra, 10 pods, 100 g	85	20
Olive, see fruit		
Onion, average, 100 g	105	25
½ cup, chopped, 60 g	65	16
Fried rings, plain, 20 g	270	65
Frozen, boiled, 60 g	60	15
Spring, 1 stalk, 10 g	10	2
Parsley, 1 tbsp chopped, 10 g	5	1
Parsnip, ½ medium, 50 g	105	25
Peas, green, ½ cup, 60 g	150	36
Canned, ½ cup, 60 g	160	37
Dried, ½ cup, boiled, 60 g	115	27
Frozen, ½ cup, boiled, 60 g	125	29
Snow peas, 10 pods, 35 g	50	10
Split peas, see **Pulses and Beans**		
Potato, average, 100 g	280	67
Baby, 25 g	70	17
Gourmet, 50 g	140	33
Small, 100 g	280	67
Medium, 150 g	430	100
Large, 200 g	560	135
Extra large, 300 g	840	200
New, canned, 100 g	240	56
Baked in jacket, 1 medium, 150 g	455	110

	kJ	Cals
If filling your baked potatoes, add the kilojoules of the ingredients. See also **Take-Away Foods**		
Hash Browns, ½ cup, 100 g	1100	265
Mashed, dried, 100 g	380	91
100 g with 2 tbsp milk and 4 g butter	510	120
Roasted, 1 tbsp fat, 4 pieces, 100 g	660	160
1 whole, 100 g	500	120
Sauteed, 100 g slices	490	115
Potato chips, per 100 g, average, uncooked,	630	150
Crinkle cut, deep fried	1220	290
Straight cut, deep fried	1060	255
Shoestring chips, deep fried	1350	325
Potato gems, uncooked, 100 g	820	195
Fried, 100 g	1030	246
Potato salad, average, ½ cup	550	130
See also **Salads and Salad Dressings**		
Pumpkin, butternut, raw, peeled, 50 g	90	21
Common, Queensland blue, raw, peeled, 100 g	185	45
Mashed, milk and butter, 50 g	150	35

	kJ	Cals
Roasted, 1 tbsp oil, 50 g	205	50
Nuggett, raw, peeled, 50 g	60	14
whole, 500 g with skin	420	100
Radish, average, 1 small, 20 g	10	2
Sauerkraut, canned, ⅔ cup, 100 g	90	22
Seaweed, fresh, 100 g	130	30
Dried, 10 g	110	25
Shallots, 20 g	20	5
Silverbeet, 50 g	25	6
Sorrel, 1 cup, 50 g	60	15
Soybeans, cooked, ½ cup, 100 g	450	110
Soybean products, see **Pulses and Beans**		
Spaghetti vegetable, ½ cup, 100 g	125	30
Spinach, average, ½ cup cooked, 100 g	65	15
Frozen, ½ cup cooked, 100 g	90	21
Sprouts, see alfalfa		
Squash, average, 3 button, 50 g	50	12
Swede, ⅙ whole, 50 g	40	10
Sweet potato, average, ¼ small, 100 g		
Purple skinned	350	85
White flesh	250	60
Yellow flesh	300	70
Sweetcorn, 1 medium cob, 100 g	250	60
1 large cob, 200 g	520	125

	kJ	Cals
Canned kernels, 100 g	395	96
Canned, creamed, 100 g	340	81
Frozen kernels, boiled, 100 g	425	103
Frozen cobs, boiled, ½ cob, 125 g	360	86
Tamarillo, 1 medium, 60 g	65	15
Taro, ¾ cup when diced, 100 g	440	105
Tomato, 1 medium, 100 g	55	13
Cherry tomatoes, 4 small, 25 g	15	3
Roma, egg, 1 medium, 60 g	40	10
Teardrop, 4 small, 30 g	15	3
Canned, 100 g	80	19
Puree, ½ cup, 100 g	120	29
Paste, 1 tbsp, 13 g	35	8
Turnip, 1 medium, 100 g	80	19
Turnip greens, 1 bunch, 50 g	45	10
Water chestnuts, 8 whole, 50 g	130	30
Watercress, 20 sprigs, 20 g	15	4
Yam, ⅔ cup, 100 g	510	122
Zucchini, 1 average, ⅔ cup sliced		
Golden	70	17
Green	155	13

PICKLED VEGETABLES

	kJ	Cals
Baby cucumbers, 1 whole, 50 g	105	25
Capers, 1 tbsp, 30 g	45	10
Dill cucumbers, 1 whole, 30 g	40	10
Gherkins, 1 whole, 10 g	60	15
Italian vegetable mix, average, 50 g	50	12
Onions, average, 1 medium, 50 g	150	35

SPECIALTY FROZEN VEGETABLES

BIRDS EYE (per 100 g)

	kJ	Cals
Beans, butter	80	19
Cross cut	140	34
Whole baby	140	34
With carrots and corn	185	44
With corn	225	54
Capsicum	75	18
Carrots, baby	130	31
Diced	100	24
Rings	100	24
With cauliflower and broccoli	95	22
Chunky vegetable mix	125	30
Garden gourmet vegetables, with cheese sauce	360	87
With herb sauce	125	30
With Thai sauce	235	56
With tomato sauce	265	63

	kJ	Cals
Green dragon, Cantonese	245	58
Chow mein	130	31
Sweet and sour	130	31
Thai vegetables	270	65
Mixed vegetables	140	34
Onion, chopped	100	24
Sliced	100	24
Peas, with beans and corn	230	55
With carrot and cauliflower	140	34
With corn and capsicum	285	68
With mint	265	63
Potatoes		
Bacon flavoured gems	800	190
Barbeque flavoured gems	800	190
Bubble and squeak	340	80
Cheese and onion flavoured gems	800	190
Crinkle cut oven fries (no cholesterol)	580	139
Homestyle chips	590	141
Microwiz chips	850	203
Ovenfry gems	800	190
Shoestring chips	665	158
Shoestring chips (no cholesterol)	765	182
Straight ovenfries	590	141
Sweetcorn, cobettes	370	88
Little ears	370	88
Sunny cobs	370	88

INDEX

127